GW00569329

❧ WICCA ☙

Inspiring | Educating | Creating | Entertaining

Brimming with creative inspiration, how-to projects, and useful information to enrich your everyday life, quarto.com is a favorite destination for those pursuing their interests and passions.

First published in 2022 by Wellfleet Press,
an imprint of The Quarto Group,
142 West 36th Street, 4th Floor,
New York, NY 10018, USA
T (212) 779-4972 F (212) 779-6058
www.Quarto.com

Wellfleet titles are also available at discount for retail, wholesale, promotional, and bulk purchase. For details, contact the Special Sales Manager by email at specialsales@quarto.com or by mail at The Quarto Group, Attn: Special Sales Manager, 100 Cummings Center Suite, 265D, Beverly, MA 01915 USA.

10 9 8 7 6 5 4 3 2 1

Library of Congress Control Number: 2021947785

ISBN: 978-1-57715-262-0

Publisher: Rage Kindelsperger
Creative Director: Laura Drew
Editor: Elizabeth You
Managing Editor: Cara Donaldson
Cover and Interior Design: Ashley Prine/Tandem Books

Printed in China

IN FOCUS

WICCA

Your Personal Guide

Tracie Long

WELLFLEET
PRESS

CONTENTS

INTRODUCTION

Welcome to the fascinating world of Wicca. Wicca is a path of transformation and growth that will challenge you and lead you to a renewed and enriched life. The most important things to remember if you decide to take this path are to read many sources so you keep learning; practice when possible; and pick those subjects that suit you.

Wicca refers to a modern pagan religion, meaning practitioners worship many goddesses, gods, nature, and the earth. Not all Wiccans practice witchcraft, and not all witchcraft practitioners are religious, because many follow their own path and use what resonates with them. These days Wicca refers to a set of practices, beliefs, and traditions carried out by people who call themselves Wiccans or witches, whether or not their practice includes spell casting. There are no central text, laws, or religious order, but there are some shared basic beliefs.

Wicca is based on nature and its cycles, and respect for the earth and all its creatures. It resonates with the natural forces of the universe and practitioners of Wicca see them reflected in the world around us in every person and in every living thing. Wicca is also about our place in the universe and our journey and evolution as spiritual beings; moving forward on our own personal spiritual journeys, by learning, growing, and becoming the best versions of ourselves that we can be.

Wiccans have great respect for *deity*, which means whatever god, goddess, universal, or heavenly influence aligns with each Wiccan person's beliefs. Wiccans tend to incorporate both male and female imagery, and they approach deity through many names, some familiar and others less so. They call upon both sexes of deity with ideas and images that are sometimes very ancient, and many that come from all over the world.

Witch vs. Warlock

A warlock is said to be the male version of a witch, but there has always been a debate among witches about male practitioners. Many males now prefer to be known as witches as they find the term "warlock" offensive. To many people, a witch is a witch, whatever their sex.

The relationship between a person and deity is seen as personal and subjective. Not everyone will comprehend deity in the same way, because each person is at a different point in their life, and not everyone has the same type of understanding or perspective. The most common representation of deity in the Wiccan world is probably the Triple Goddess, who has three forms: the maiden, the mother, and the crone. Her symbol is the moon, and her consort is the god who rules the cycles of the solar year; his symbol is the sun. We will discuss this goddess as well as other deities, the history of Wicca, different types of witches, several witchcraft practices, spell casting, and more in the coming chapters. After reading this book, you will know whether you feel drawn to Wicca and likely have a sense of what you want to study next on your new path.

Enclosed Wiccan Wall Chart

Included in this book is a wall chart that serves as a quick and handy reference guide, containing a summary of the essential tools of Wicca that you will learn about on the following pages.

1

WITCHCRAFT, WICCA, AND CONFUSION

When it comes to the practices of witchcraft and Wicca, there is a great deal of confusion about which witch is which. These "crafts" can both be one and the same, or they can be very different from each other. Followers of the various crafts can work together by meeting in groups or by using online methods to communicate with one another. They may use similar terminology and celebrate their craft in a similar way.

Other practitioners work alone, and each individual may perform their craft in a different way from other solitary witches, whether they are Wiccan or not. These folks may be so different from one another in the way they work that they don't understand each other's jargon or the first thing about the rituals others perform. A surprising number of Wiccans make up their own rules as they go along.

Because there are so many types of witches, some of whom are Wiccan and some of whom aren't, using the terms "witch" and "Wiccan" can be very confusing.

Witchcraft is many things, as it can be part of a pagan religion, in which different gods and goddesses were (and still are) worshipped. It can encompass healing for people, animals, and the land; it can include attempts to control the weather; it can entail casting spells and divining the future. Witchcraft was even used with a fair bit of success in the UK during World War II, when a group of witches gathered in England to raise a cone of power to aid in stopping Hitler from invading after France fell. It is accepted in some places and some cultures and disliked in others. We still use the term "a witch hunt" to describe a concerted effort by some self-styled authority to destroy a person or a reputation, or perhaps wipe out some sector of society.

Witchcraft has a very long history in the UK and Europe, which adds to the confusion. It exists in some form in every country of the world, perhaps

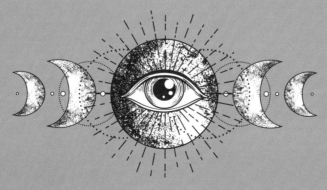

as shamanism, trance healing, finding lost objects, and performing rituals for a myriad of reasons—including unpleasant ones. However, Wicca itself is modern, and while it is similar to traditional witchcraft, it is not the same. Let's look at some of the history behind witchcraft and then Wicca.

The Persecutions

Over many centuries, witches have been the heart of many cultures. In some villages they were known as wise women, medicine women, healers, and midwives. The whole village would call upon them for their help. Functioning as a form of doctor, they were greatly respected and an integral part of the community. But when villages or even countries faced hardships, such as war or food shortages, people would sometimes turn on local practitioners and accuse them of evil deeds. The infamous "witch hunts" are examples of this and constitute

Queen Elizabeth I

a dark period in history. Below are a few of the problems that governments and officials caused in the past, which usually affected those who had nothing to do with witchcraft—and certainly nothing to do with black magic or the so-called black arts, which is associated with the devil or evil spirits.

The Witchcraft Act

In England, the Witchcraft Act of 1563 was passed under Queen Elizabeth I, in which it was said that anyone who "practiced or exercised any Witchcraft, Enchantment, Charm or Sorcery, where any person happened to be killed or destroyed was found guilty of a felony, and without the benefit of clergy would be put to death."

In 1604, King James I expanded the act to bring the penalty of death to anyone who invoked evil spirits or communed with *familiar spirits*. (*Familiar spirits* or *familiars* were spirits that supposedly helped the so-called witch.) These people were considered so evil that they couldn't be saved, so they were tried without the "benefit of clergy," meaning they were tried by a secular court instead of the Church's. It was this amendment that was then enforced by the notorious Matthew Hopkins, who became known as the Witch-finder General. He sentenced many innocent people accused of witchcraft to death, and these people were routinely denied an opportunity to confess their sins and be absolved of them before their execution.

The Salem Trials

Across the ocean to colonial America, a panic about alleged witchcraft broke out in the late 1600s. In Salem, Massachusetts, Betty Parris, the daughter of Reverend Samuel Parris, and her cousin Abigail Williams began to act strangely, speaking oddly, hiding things, and creeping about. None of their doctors could tell what was wrong with the girls, and some concluded that it was the hand of the evil that was on them; in other words they were possessed. The Reverend Parris, together with other upstanding citizens, and Betty and

A scene from the Salem Witch Trials

The Witchcraft Act of 1735

⋯•••◆◆◆◆•••⋯

In the UK, the Witchcraft Act of 1735 was repealed in 1951, largely at the instigation of spiritualist organizations who were finding themselves hampered by the act, despite having nothing to do with any form of witchcraft. One law that still exists today in the UK makes it illegal to give any kind of reading in the street or in an outdoor public place, other than in a properly organized psychic event. This is why you never see people reading fortunes in the street in the UK.

Abigail, along with several other so-called possessed children—Ann Putnam, Betty Hubbard, Mercy Lewis, Susannah Sheldon, Mercy Short, and Mary Warren—began accusing others of witchcraft, leading to a series of trials and subsequent executions.

As the number of accusations grew, the jail population of Salem also grew. Those who were accused but not yet arrested gathered their belongings and fled far away, some as far as New York. The witch trials ended in January 1693, when a new act stated that, "It was better that any unsuspected witches should escape than the innocent person should be condemned." Today the rule is still "innocent until proven guilty."

Modern Witchcraft

Witchcraft as we know it today comes down to two men, Gerald Gardner and Alexander Sanders, who researched and revived it in the 1950s and 1960s. Modern witchcraft has rules, rituals, adherence to the ceremonies at various times of the year, standards or "degrees" that a trainee works toward, and its own beliefs. Another writer, Aleister Crowley, researched and wrote about witchcraft, including magic and alchemy, among many things, but he also embraced rumors that he was a Satanist.

Wicca in the Modern World

So, to reiterate, some Wiccans are indistinguishable from traditional witches because they follow the yearly ceremonies, worship pagan gods, and use ancient rituals. Some Wiccans form small groups of like-minded people, while others work entirely alone. Some follow common religions, such as Christianity or Judaism, while others have no allegiance to any religion at all. Some use candle spells commonly with prayers and hoped-for blessings rather than anything overtly witchy.

Modern Wiccans are frequently women, grown out of a yearning for women to have something of their own. The major world religions are male-dominated, and extreme elements have made the lives of many women difficult, if not almost impossible. Wicca is a quieter, gentler space that women can inhabit in peace. Wicca isn't reserved for women, though, and all types of people are welcome to

THE ROOTS OF THE CRAFT

Gerald Gardner called his beliefs and methods Wicca, but he also referred to his creation as "The Craft." He popularized his form of Wicca in the New Forest in the south of England, and his followers, including Doreen Valiente, Patricia Crowther, and Eleanor Bone, spread his ideas round the UK and into other English-speaking countries. Others came along and created spin-offs of the original, including Robert Cochrane, Sybil Leek, and Alexander Sanders. New organizations, such as the Witchcraft Research Association, came into being. In the United States, a new form of Wicca arrived, Dianic Wicca, and an organization called the Covenant of the Goddess was formed.

Internationally, the 200-coven-strong Fellowship of Isis exists worldwide. At one time, it included in the upper levels of its hierarchy the distinguished author Ralph Harvey. He wrote about the revival of witchcraft in Sussex in the UK in *The Last Bastion*, which has been republished as an e-book, *British Witchcraft*.

Just to show how diverse all this is, during the 1960s, Sybil Leek, who was a follower of Gardner, wrote excellent books on astrology without a mention of witchcraft or Wicca in them—and she wasn't alone in that. Madeline Montalban was a ceremonial magician who founded the Order of the Morning Star and promoted her own form of Luciferianism. She was associated with Gardner, Sanders, and Crowley, and she was a prolific writer on the tarot, astrology, and other esoteric subjects, but you would never have known from Montalban's writing that she was also a witch. It seems that people can wear a variety of hats within the world of witchcraft and Wicca.

follow the Wiccan way of life. Many celebrate Wiccan holidays, known as sabbats, if only by making a nice meal for themselves and their friends.

Who Are the Wiccans?

Wiccans are gentle people who honor the earth and do their best to avoid harming it. All those whom I have met love animals and wouldn't even kill a spider. Some believe in the Hindu and Buddhist ideas of karma and reincarnation, but others do not. Some believe that this life is a learning process that helps our spirits to grow, rather than a place in which we can expect to be happy all the time. Some dislike materialism. All Wiccans share a belief that bad deeds come back on us more strongly than when they are sent out, and that helps Wiccans to stay on the straight and narrow.

Some are great gardeners, and those who are into complementary therapy love to grow their own herbs and use kitchen-cupboard remedies for minor complaints. Some love to dress up in "witchy" outfits and attend witchy or fairy festivals, while others do not. Some love to grow their hair long and wear crowns of flowers on special occasions, while others would feel silly doing such a thing. Some wear a pentacle or a crystal to express their spirituality, and others do not. Many are into angels and archangels, and there are now several forms of angelic Wicca. Most perform some form of ritual and spell casting, especially when they or their friends need a bit of extra help from the universe.

All love crystals, candles, spells, and herbs, and many bring the elements to bear on their spell casting. Many burn incense, send good vibes, and try to live as decent human beings. All are pretty psychic, and every Wiccan that I know loves to give readings by means of tarot, astrology, the runes, palmistry, or spiritual channeling. Like many Romany people, Wiccans can be wonderfully accurate diviners of the future, as well as terrific healers and counselors.

The Different Types of Witches and Wicca

Many different types of witches have developed over the centuries and in the modern world of Wicca. They believe similar things but practice how they feel best suits them. Take a look at the list of some of the types and see which approach resonates with you.

Gardnerian Witches

Gardnerian witchcraft was started in the 1950s by Gerald Gardner. He was the first to publicize witchcraft to preserve the old ways. Gardner was initiated into a coven of witches in the New Forest region of England in 1939 by a high priestess named Old Dorothy Clutterbuck.

In 1949, Gerald wrote a novel called *High Magic's Aid*, about medieval witchcraft. He later wrote a second book called *Witchcraft Today* and founded modern Wicca. Gardnerian covens are always headed by a high priestess, and they have three degrees of initiation that are centered on the Goddess and the Horned God. Traditionally the idea is based on fertility, and the cycle of birth, death, and rebirth. The system includes the eight seasonal sabbats, meditation, chanting, astral projection, cord magic, and other subjects that we will cover later in this book. Gardnerian witchcraft is designed for group or coven work, and the covens would work *sky-clad*, or naked.

Which Witch?

Everyone interested in Wicca should feel empowered to do their own thing as long as they remember not to harm anyone or anything.

Alexandrian Witches

The Alexandrian organization was founded during the 1960s by Alexander Sanders, one of Gardner's early initiates and a self-proclaimed king of the witches. Alexandrian witches' covens tend to focus on training that's associated with ceremonial magic, such as Qabalah, angelic magic, and Enochian magic. The Alexandrian coven has a hierarchical structure. The groups meet weekly or at least on full moons, new moons, and the sabbats. Their rituals are usually done sky-clad. Most Alexandrian covens allow outsiders to attend their circles, although usually someone who has some basic training in the craft prior to being accepted for the first-degree initiation.

Augury Witches

The Augury are like shamans, as they will help to direct those on a spiritual quest by interpreting the signs and symbols that they encounter. The term *Augury* originates from the Roman augurs, whose purpose was to discover whether the gods approved of a proposed course of action, by interpreting signs or omens such as the appearance of animals that were sacred to the gods. Augury witches are not seen as fortune tellers; their gifts are mainly of heaven-sent prophecy rather than divination.

Celtic Witches

Celtic Wicca focuses mainly on Celtic and Druidic gods and goddesses. Their rituals are more like those of the Gardnerian tradition, with an emphasis on nature and working with elementals and nature spirits such as fairies, tree spirits, and gnomes.

Ceremonial Witches

Ceremonial witchcraft is focused on rituals that are usually followed "by the book," meaning precisely and with a lot of ceremony. Ceremonial practitioners may use a combination of disciplines drawn from tradition, but they often employ scientific precision such as sacred mathematics and quantum mysticism. They also call upon spiritual entities and archetypal figures representative of the energies they wish to manifest.

Eclectic Witches

This term often refers to groups and individuals who do not follow one specific form of Wicca or witchcraft. They choose to incorporate beliefs, practices, and rituals of many paths to form a unique system that suits their spiritual needs. They do not follow a particular religion or tradition, but study and learn from many different techniques, and they use what works best for them.

Elemental Witches

This type of witch works with the four elements—water, earth, air, and fire—or five, adding spirit. They dedicate different areas of their altars to each element and call upon them during spell work and rituals.

Faery Witches

Faery witches like to commune with the faery folk and nature spirits in their magic workings. They have no organization or tradition, and their belief has developed of its own accord through common practice. They tend to incorporate their own poetry, music, and invocations into their rituals.

Green Witches

The aim of the green witch is to achieve magic through communion with Mother Nature, and by using her energies, along with natural items; green witches visit calming, peaceful places such as fields or forests, which allow them to be closer to nature.

Hedge Witches

Hedge-craft is earth-based spirituality. The term *hedge* signified the boundary of the village and represents the boundary that exists between this world and the spiritual realm. These witches tend to be powerful healers and midwives. A bird is usually associated with the hedge witch, most commonly the raven and the goose. These witches prefer to work alone.

Hereditary Witches

Also known as a *family tradition witch*, this is someone who has been taught the Old Ways passed down through the generations of their family. Though one may be born into a family with the tradition, nobody is born a witch, so a conscious decision and an acceptance of the Craft is necessary for someone to become a witch.

Kitchen Witches (Also Known as Cottage Witches)

This practitioner of witchcraft uses the tools of hearth and home to work their spells and create their own rituals. A kitchen witch also deals with the practical sides of religion, magic, and the elements of the earth. This is now a popular type of witchcraft, as it is about working with the energies of nature to make the hearth and home a secure and sacred place.

Solitary Witch

This is one who practices alone, without a coven and without following any tradition. This witch mixes different systems, much like eclectic witches. They tend to form their own religious beliefs because they are not bound by the rules of a coven.

Secular Witches

Secular witches do not connect with deities in their magic or rituals. They believe the energy comes from the earth and its natural resources, and they use herbs, plants, crystals, and stones in their practice.

Wiccan Witches

Wicca has a good balance between religion and ceremonial magic and nature. Wiccans believe in a god and goddess who are equal in all things. They often form covens and rarely like to work alone.

Going Forward

Who knows where Wicca will be a century from now? Something of the kind will still exist, though, because it always has. We all need a bit of help from time to time, and standard religion doesn't work for everyone, so maybe the gentle, feminine world of Wicca will still be the road to peace and happiness for many people.

So mote it be.

❈ ❈ ❈

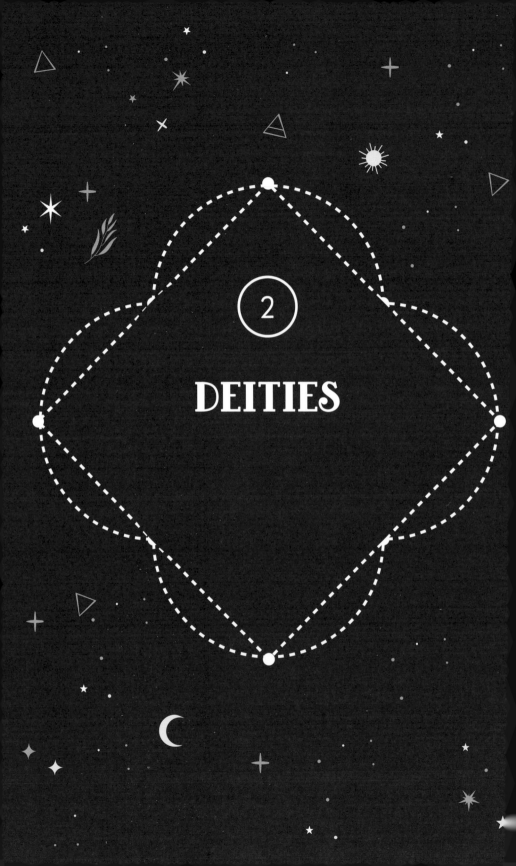

2

DEITIES

Wiccans believe in an ultimate power, spirit, or force that can't be touched. This power, spirit, or force encompasses the whole universe: the moon, the sun, stars, and planets.

Wiccans believe this divine energy manifests in the forms of a goddess and god that they are able to communicate with. As both deities emanate from the same source, both retain equal power, hence equal status. By manifesting the power in two deities, the divine retains the natural balance of opposites: male and female, summer and winter, light and dark, and life and death. Each opposite is essential to maintaining the balance and rhythm of life. During ritual ceremonies and magic work, Wiccans can call on many deities that come from different cultures and periods in history but all of whom are, in essence, merely different aspects of the same goddess and god, of the universal divine energy.

The Triple Goddess and the Horned God

In Wicca, the archetype of the female deity is the Triple Goddess, who has three forms: the maiden, the mother, and the crone. Her symbol is the moon. Her consort is the Horned God, who rules the cycles of the solar year. His symbol is known as the sun. The Triple Goddess is an archetype embodying all the aspects of the goddesses instead of one specific goddess, though the Greek goddess Hecate is often thought to be the original Triple Goddess. The Horned God is her male counterpart, and while he too is a bit of an archetype for the father god, he is often thought to be the Celtic god Cernunnos.

These two figures are the main deities in Wicca, but Wiccans also worship individual goddesses and gods that have different, particular characteristics and powers. In a way, these specific deities are aspects of the Triple Goddess and the Horned God.

The Goddesses

A goddess is a divine female being of supernatural powers or attributes, whom people believe in and worship. A goddess is often believed to be the source of life and is worshipped as the principal deity in various religions. For thousands of years, people around the world have worshipped a divine and powerful mother-goddess who has been honored as the mother of all life.

To some, the goddess is not confined to human form, as many cultures perceive her to be the goddess within nature, who lives in plants, trees, mountains, and stars, each of which is inhabited by a unique goddess spirit. For every star that dies, another is being formed in the universe; for each plant or tree that dies, another is waiting to be reborn in the seeds of the previous one. Thus, the spirit of the goddess becomes immortal, because energy always exists in many forms.

To others, the goddess is transcendent and exists outside us, where the goddess becomes the universe, so she may be known as Gaia, Mother Nature, the Great Goddess, or the Great Mother. The transcendent goddess is vast, timeless, and immortal, being a spirit that is always everywhere.

Many who walk the path of the goddess believe that the goddess within can be called upon for strength and guidance whenever we face the challenges of life. The goddess dwells within all of us, and she is the small voice of conscience, through whom we find a connection to the divine within ourselves, seeking the strength of the goddess within to improve our lives. Contact with the goddess can be a transformative, enlightening, and empowering experience.

Modern Goddess and God Worship in Wicca

Many modern witches view Mother Earth as a biological system, and they believe that we all depend upon one another for survival. The goddess is the giver of all life and is found in all of creation.

The goddess is important to both men and women, because she allows men to acknowledge the feminine energies within themselves and to accept their desire and need of a protective, nurturing feminine presence. The image of the goddess inspires women to see themselves as divine, to see their bodies as

sacred, and to view the changing phases of life as holy. Through the goddess, we can discover our strength, enlighten our minds, own our bodies, and celebrate our emotions.

Seeking the goddess through Wicca is the beginning of a journey that brings balance to the female and male energies, so it is natural to want to balance our spiritual lives. By accepting the goddess and god, we start our inner journey to discover our "higher self." This higher self is often referred to as the "god self," and it is the path to deep wisdom.

Below is a list of ancient goddesses and gods who are most often associated with Wicca and witchcraft. There are thousands of goddesses from many different cultures, so you must find the ones that you feel most comfortable with.

Brigid

The Celtic goddess of fire, fertility, cattle, crops, and poetry. She is the daughter of Dagda (see page 26), and her name means "the exalted one." Her festival is the celebration of the Imbolc, the fire festival sabbat that falls on February 1st (see page 58 for more).

Cerridwen

The Celtic goddess associated with cauldrons and the underworld. She can change shape into various animals, such as the greyhound, otter, hawk, and hen. Her name refers to the color white, and she is sometimes called the White One or White Grain. Many consider her a moon goddess.

Goddess Cerridwen can take the shape of a hawk.

Flidais

The Celtic woodland goddess of wild creatures and sex. Her name means "deer," and she is also referred to as the Mistress of Stags. She is said to be accompanied by a magical cow, whose milk can sustain hundreds.

Freya

Freya is the Norse goddess of fertility.
The ancient Romans associated her
with Venus, the goddess of love.

Norse goddess Freya

Hecate

The ancient Greek goddess of the
moon, the underworld, enchantment,
and night spirits. Hecate belongs
to the class of goddesses known as
"the torchbearers." Such goddesses
possessed the knowledge of the spirit
realms and held the secrets of nature
in their hands. She was also known as
Anthea, the sender of night visions.
She is usually portrayed as triple-faced,
representing the maiden, mother, and
crone, and the phases of the moon.

Jana

As the ancient Roman goddess of
doorways, entrances, and portals, Jana
bears the key to unlocking other realms,
which also associates her with the
underworld and other worlds.

The Horae

These ancient Greek deities, Thallo, Auxo,
and Carpo, are of a threefold nature. They
relate to the seasons and plant growth.

Ancient Greek goddess Hecate

Thallo represents blooming plants, Auxo symbolizes growth, while Carpo
represents crops in their maturity. The word "Horae" is derived from the Greek
word for time or hours, thus the period of growth and maturity. The Horae
were deities of agriculture who attended to the Harvest Lord in his time.

The Gods

While goddesses feature more prominently in Wicca, the gods are also important and embody certain features and powers that are important for the cycle of nature, rituals, and spells. The following is a list of the best-known Wiccan gods.

Cernunnos

The Celtic god of the forest, fertility, and the hunt takes the form of a man with the horns of a stag. He is the universal father, sometimes having three heads. In Wicca, he is the consort of the Triple Goddess, and he is often called upon during Wiccan rituals.

Celtic god Cernunnos.

Arawn

The Welsh god of the underworld and the dead.

Dagda

The Irish god associated with fertility, agriculture, and strength, as well as magic, druidry, and wisdom.

Frey

The Norse god of fertility. His worshippers incorporate phallic images into their rites.

Herne

The horned British spirit known as Herne the Hunter is associated with the wild hunt. He is often depicted wearing deerskins and a crown of stag's antlers, similar to Cernunnos.

Mars

The ancient Roman god of war and agriculture. Dressed in armor and carrying a shield, he has companion animals including a wolf, a woodpecker, and a vulture.

Janus

The ancient Roman god of beginnings, transitions, and doorways is depicted as a bearded man with two faces: one looks to the past, and the other looks to the future. He can see the inside and outside of all things at the same time.

Ogma

The Irish and Scottish god of language and inspiration. He takes the form of a wise old man. He wears animal skins, and gold chains pour out of his mouth. He also invented the druid alphabet.

Ancient Greek god Janus

3

WICCAN SYMBOLS

There are a number of symbols that stand for important concepts for Wiccans and witches, and some believe these symbols themselves contain a certain amount of power.

The Pentagram

The most common symbol is the pentagram, which is the five-pointed star inside a circle. (When the symbol adorns a physical object, it is called a pentacle, which you'll learn about in the chapter on witches' tools.) It attracts a lot of negative attention because most people don't really know what it means or what it symbolizes and wrongly associate it with devil worship (which uses it inverted).

The pentagram is in fact a universal symbol of paganism, Wicca, and witchcraft. Each of the five points represents one of the four elements, with the fifth—the top point—representing spirit in general or one's own spirit, depending upon the particular witch's point of view. The circle links all five points together, representing ourselves and the fact that we are all part of one unity. The pentagram also stands for the element of earth on its own, and it can be used to represent earth on an altar.

Though the pentagram is perhaps the symbol most people can recognize as having to do with magic, it is far from the only one used by Wiccans. Here is a short guide to some of the other powerful symbols used in witchcraft.

Ankh

The ankh originated in ancient Egypt and stands for the key of life or eternal life and immortality. This is an optimistic symbol that also relates to fertility, creativity, and longevity.

Septagram

The septagram is a seven-pointed star. It is similar to the pentagram but with two more points. The septagram has a spiritual meaning because the number seven is connected to the astral or fairy realm. The points represent the four elements, with the additional points representing above, below, and within. It is sometimes drawn with a circle joining all the points, but not always.

Hexagram

The hexagram is not as well known as other symbols. It is sometimes called a unicursal hexagram because it's a six-pointed star, but it is one that can be drawn as one continuous line rather than using two triangles as in a star of David. Like the other star symbols, the number of points has its own meaning, with six standing for balance and continuity.

Green Man

Known as a nature spirit, the Green Man has leafy features, often with vegetation emerging from his mouth. In Wicca he is seen as both an aspect of the god and an aspect of the environment. He is also associated with the Beltane festival and the coming of summer.

Cornucopia

This is the horn of plenty, and it is the symbol of the ancient Roman goddess Ceres, the goddess of fertility and abundance. It can be worn as a symbol or as a wish for abundance.

Eight-Spoked Wheel

A symbol of the sacred year, as each spoke represents one of the seasonal sabbats. It is also the wheel of Fortuna, the goddess of chance and fate in the Roman pantheon.

Threes

Threes are important in Wicca. Triangles, triskeles, and Celtic knots all resonate with the mathematical and geometric philosophies of the ancient Greeks and the spiritual symbols used by the Celts. Triskeles are three-legged swirls representing the power of earth, water, and fire. Celtic knots are loops made from one thread to represent eternity, also associated with loyalty, faith, friendship, or love.

Triquetra

This Celtic symbol represents the sacred number three. There are many things that three symbolizes, with the obvious one being manifestation, because humans, animals, fish, and even plants need a male and female to create offspring. There are also the elements of sky, land, and sea, as well as, in Christianity, the Holy Trinity.

Triple Moon

This symbol is popular; it shows the three main phases of the moon: waxing, full, and waning. It also represents the three phases of the goddess—the maiden, mother, and crone. It is also a Wiccan symbol of the sacred feminine.

Webs

These are important symbols in contemporary Wicca because they describe the way we consider the spiritual and physical universe and the magic of nature.

Mazes and Labyrinths

Mazes are symbols of left-brain function because they represent logic and reason. A labyrinth depicts the journey from birth, through life, to death and rebirth. Labyrinths are found in many cultures and marked on ancient monuments around the world.

4

WITCHES' TOOLS

Witches have a wide range of magical tools that are used for rituals. Each item has a purpose and represents the different elements, aspects, or associations to the rituals or spells they wish to perform.

Book of Shadows

The book of shadows is the name for a book that a witch creates. It can be used to record spells, but it can also contain all manner of notes that a witch would like to have on hand for reference. Witches like to record the spells they have performed so they can check back on the results, but many also include in their book their dreams, visions, meditations, rituals, and their tarot readings, a bit like a diary. Your own book of shadows can be any size, shape, or color, so long as it appeals to you. Traditionally, the book of shadows was handwritten, but today's books are often typed, and poems and other entries can be copied into it.

KEEPING A DETAILED JOURNAL

Recording your spells, rituals, and workings, will be helpful later when you are trying to determine what does and does not work for you, and how you may want to change things at a later date.

- First write out your ritual and its purpose.
- Add the date and time of when you performed the ritual.
- Make a note of the moon phase and any astrological references, depending on how you work with these.
- List the tools and other items you used.
- Name the god or goddess invoked, if any.
- Note how long the ritual or spell took to prepare and perform.
- Write up any results of the ritual or spell casting.

The term "shadows" means the notes about spells and workings, but the whole spell is not written out. A spell contains real energy, so the notes are a *shadow* of the real work. You should try to write down notes on everything you do and make a record of the use to which you put your spells or rituals. The idea is to make notes so that you understand the spell and how to perform it but no one else would be able to copy or use it, as spells are deeply personal.

The Athame

The athame (pronounced ath-*aim*) is a traditional ritual dagger that often has a black handle and a double-edged steel blade. The athame is used  to direct whatever power you pass through it, to cast circles by tracing the circumference of an area, to charge objects with energy, to consecrate objects, and to banish negative energies. It's only ever used for magical purposes and never on a person or for harm. It is an elemental tool, sometimes associated with the element of fire, but in other traditions it is associated with the element of air. The phallic symbolism of the knife links it with the energy of a Wiccan god.

THE WICCAN REDE

The Wiccan Rede is the closest thing in Wicca to being a law. The Rede is a testament to what Wiccans stand for. What follows is the short form of this testament. You can add this to your book of shadows so that you can recite it when you do a ritual, which may come in handy when you can't think of anything else to say.

Abide the Wiccan law ye must,
In perfect love and perfect trust,
Eight words the Wiccan Rede fulfil,
An' it harms none, do as ye will,
And ever mind the rule of three,
What ye send out comes back to thee,
Follow this with mind and heart,
And merry ye meet and merry ye part.

The message here is to do whatever ritual or spell you like, as long as it is not designed to harm anyone. If someone has behaved badly toward you, it is best to allow fate to take care of them and leave it at that. Wiccans honestly believe that if you curse someone, you will receive bad luck that is three times as nasty as whatever you sent out. If you set out to help others, though, this will also come back to you threefold, so be sure that you only send out positive vibes. If you find this hard to do, especially under difficult circumstances, don't perform magic on those who are hurting you but try working on yourself instead.

The Pentacle

The pentacle is a traditional tool of witchcraft. It is usually a round, solid disc that can be made from metal, stone, wood, or copper. The disc is engraved or painted with an upright five-pointed star that is enclosed inside a circle. The symbol itself is called a pentagram, while an object bearing the symbol is a pentacle. It is normally the centerpiece of the altar.

The Wand

The wand is one of the main tools of witchcraft.
It should be approximately the length of the
inside of your arm, from the crook of the elbow
to the middle of your index finger. If you want to
make your own wand, you can choose any tree you like, cut the wood, and thank
the tree for its gift. These days, many materials besides wood are used, and
some wands are tipped with crystals and gems. The wand is a tool of invocation
that is used to evoke gods, goddesses, and spirits; bestow blessings; and charge
objects with energy during a ritual. In most traditions the wand represents the
element of air, but in some it represents the element of fire.

The Censer

The censer is an incense burner that is used to hold burning
incense during a ritual. Any type of censer can be used; even
a simple bowl filled with sand will do. The censer
represents the element of air, and it is normally
placed before the images of the goddess and god
on the altar.

The Chalice

The chalice is an elemental tool that represents
water. The base is symbolic of the material world,
the stem of the connection between man and spirit,
and the rim or opening receives spiritual energy.
As a whole, it is a symbol of containment and often
represents the womb of the goddess.

    The chalice can be made of any material. In
ancient times, horns, shells, and gourds were used
to hold sacred liquids during rituals, and then in later times, silver became the
preferred material. The chalice is used to hold blessed water and wine during a
ritual, similar to the Eucharist in Christianity. It is traditional in many covens
to pass the chalice around so all members can take a drink as a token of unity.
It's also associated with the moon and the goddess.

The Broom

The broom is a ritual tool that is sacred to both the goddess
and the god. For the god its phallic shape is symbolic. For the
goddess, it's made up of three pieces—the stick, brush, and the
binding cord—which relate to the triple nature of the female
deity. Traditionally, the broom is made from three different
woods: ash for the handle, birch twigs for the brush, and
willow for the binding cord. The broom is used for a variety
of purposes, such as ritually cleansing an area before magic is
performed by symbolically sweeping away negative energies. It
was once used to guard the home against psychic attack or evil curses by
placing it across the threshold, on windowsills, or in doorways. I have one near
my doorway and these days I use it as part of pagan wedding ceremonies called
handfastings, which include a broom jump.

The Bolline

The bolline is a white-handled knife that is used
to harvest herbs; its blade is shaped like a small
sickle. You can find these knives in gardening shops,
where they are called pruning knives. It has a white
handle to differentiate it from the athame. In addition to
cutting herbs, the bolline is used to cut wands, to mark and
carve candles with symbols, and to cut cords for use in magic. Any ritual that
involves cutting or carving can be performed using this knife, such as cutting
flowers for the altar, but you shouldn't use it for general gardening purposes.

The Cauldron

In ancient times the cauldron was used as a cooking
vessel and for brew making. It was made from cast
iron, resting on three legs and with an opening
smaller than its widest part.

Today it is used as a container in rituals for
making brews and potions, or to contain a small fire
for use with spells. It is symbolic of the womb of the
goddess and is the manifested essence of femininity and fertility. It is symbolic
of the element of water, and it is linked with the ideas of reincarnation,

immortality, and inspiration. It can also be used for scrying, or foretelling the future, by filling it with water and gazing into its depths.

The Bell

The bell is a ritual tool of invocation and banishment that can be rung before the ritual begins to indicate the start of a rite to drive off negative influences. It is frequently used to invoke the goddess during rituals or sounded at the four quarters (north, south, east, and west) to call forth such spirits as the watchers and elementals. (See page 45 for more on this.) Bells can be used to guard the home by warding off evil spirits or evoking good energies when hung on doors.

Witches' Keys

Keys are old tools that are used in magic, and they can be used for divination and ritual purposes. They symbolize the power to change reality and open doors to the other realms. A witch might use an old key to help her travel through spiritual realms and to seek the guidance of higher and wiser entities. Once activated, the key can be used to summon spirits without the witch having to make a great deal of effort. Keys also represent knowledge and access, so possessing a key is about gaining access and setting boundaries.

Skeleton keys (keys that can work on many locks) are often associated with specific deities or spiritual figures, and can be used as part of charms or magical tools, such as protection. Hecate, a goddess who is often described as the queen of the witches, is a deity associated with gatekeeping. She holds the keys that allow passage into the spiritual realm, and she is also a great protector. I have a few keys that I keep on a hook by my doorway to shield my home from unwanted spirits that might otherwise pass through doorways.

You can also use keys on your altar, for divination, for access to all that is unseen, as a symbol for sealed or locked away secrets, and as a talisman in a protection spell. After casting the spell, the keys can be hung at doorways for protection, but they can also be used for removing and opening blockages.

HOW TO INVOKE OR CHARGE YOUR KEY

Choose a key you are drawn to. Antique stores with old-fashioned keys are a good place to look for one. Hold your key in your hand and picture your energy and vibration mixing with the key. Call upon your guides, spirits, or angels for protection.

Say the following words out loud:

> *Sacred key, I charge you with the task of unlocking the path of mystery.*
> *Grant me pass, let me in, let me see, only me: so mote it be.*

Cords

You can cast spells by focusing and visualizing your intent and directing it onto a string or cord. Be positive about the outcome and imagine it happening, while you tie nine knots into a piece of cord, and then read out the knot spell that you'll find below.

You can make the spell stronger by using a cord that is a color associated with what you are trying to achieve. You can check out the color code in the chapter on colors and candles. (See page 88 for more on this.)

The knots should be tied in the order shown here, so start by tying knot number 1, then number 2, number 3, and so on through the sequence:

X----X----X----X----X----X----X----X----X
1   6   4   8   3   9   5   7   2

THE KNOT SPELL

> *By knot of one this string I tie,*
> *Let the magic begin, don't let it die.*
> *By knot of two it will come true,*
> *Whether I make it for me or you.*
> *By knot of three it comes to be,*
> *The magic will happen as you will see.*

By knot of four my message will soar,
Up to the gods whom we adore.
By knot of five the magic is alive,
It will happen, it will survive.
By knot of six it will be fixed,
The power increasing as the clock ticks.
By knot of seven this spell I'll leaven,
As the message is carried up to heaven.
By knot of eight it will not wait,
The magic will happen it won't be late.
By knot of nine my magic will shine,
It is my will placed in this rhyme.
So be it.

Once you have finished, place the tied cord in a safe place. If you want the magic to be permanent, bury the cord in the earth or burn it. If you keep the knotted cord, you can undo the magic whenever you like. I use mine for new ventures or positive outcomes, so I keep my cords somewhere safe.

UNDOING CORD MAGIC

Start with the last knot that you tied when you did the spell. Untie all of the knots in the opposite order to that in which you tied the cord. When all the knots are undone, your magic will stop working.

You can chant the following over and over as you untie the knots:

With each knot I untie,
Release the magic, let it fly.
And it harm none, set it free,
This is my will, so mote it be.

The order in which to untie the knots in the cord:

X----X----X-----X----X----X----X----X---X
1   6   4   8   3   9   5   7   2

Clear Quartz

This is the witch's favorite crystal, so if you are only
going to have one crystal, this is it. Clear quartz is one
of the most versatile crystals, and it is able to do just
about everything you need. It boosts the powers of
other crystals, focuses and directs energy—especially
the quartz points—and it can be used for protection, balancing, meditation,
and dispelling negative energy. I recommend you start with this one and build
up your collection. There are so many to choose from, and you will be drawn to
many of them, so it's best to invest in a good crystal guide book, such as
In Focus: Crystals, to find the best uses for each crystal.

All witches like to own a wand, and while a wand is usually made of wood
rather than crystal, a crystal can be highly effective in directing energy. Long
pieces of quartz can be used to define your circle or simply direct your energy
and desires when working.

A large piece of clear quartz can
be used as a charging crystal that
rejuvenates your other crystals and
leaves them cleansed and charged.
Quartz has protective properties, so it
can be worn close to the body either
in the form of jewelry or in a pocket
or even tucked into a bra. It can
also be placed around the home for
protection of your property.

Clear quartz can be used in a
ritual, worn as jewelry, sewn into
ritual robes, or even attached to
magical tools. It helps channel the
energy and is used for protection, to
keep negativity out, and to enhance
the safety of the circle and the
participants. You can use clear quartz
to induce prophetic dreams by putting
a piece of it beneath your pillow.

During healing, a piece of clear
quartz can be moved over the body;

Cleansing Crystals

We have to cleanse our
crystals often, and there are
many ways to cleanse and
charge them. You can use
water that has been left out
in moonlight, or you can use
moonlight itself, or sunlight,
or even bury a crystal in the
earth. One of the simplest
ways to leave crystals to
charge is to lay them on
the bed of a quartz geode
(a stone that has been cut
through to show the crystal
inside). I do this often with
the ones that I wear.

this helps to heal any weak patches in the aura, and it restores energy. When using quartz to heal, remember to cleanse your stones after use because they will pick up any residue of negativity that is clinging to the person's aura.

Your clear quartz can be infused in water and, ideally, left overnight in the full moon. The water can be used for cleansing magic tools, for clearing and blessing the home or the place of work, and for blessings in general.

Probably the most widely known use of clear quartz is the crystal ball. A crystal ball is used for divination. Some seers can see a physical image in the crystal, while others use the reflective surface. You need to focus and clear your mind and allow the images to form. They may actually form in your mind's eye rather than in the crystal itself, but the presence of the crystal helps the knowledge to come forward. This takes a lot of patience and practice, as the students in my circle will tell you!

The Altar

An altar is a sacred space or place with spiritual objects that are used for meditation, spells, rituals, divination, prayers, and connecting to the deity. It is integral to practicing Wicca.

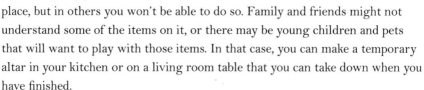

You can use any type or size table as your altar; a sideboard is often a good choice because the cabinet has shelves or drawers built in that will hold your magical supplies. Sometimes you just have to adapt to the layout in your home. In some cases, you can lay out your altar and leave it in place, but in others you won't be able to do so. Family and friends might not understand some of the items on it, or there may be young children and pets that will want to play with those items. In that case, you can make a temporary altar in your kitchen or on a living room table that you can take down when you have finished.

When you have decided on the best place to have the altar, you must decide on the tools you need and the way you want to set it up. It is traditional to set up an altar facing the north or east, but if it feels right to set up in a different direction, that's okay. Buy a nice piece of cloth in a color that you like and put it on your altar. Alternatively, you can use a white cloth, or you can choose different colors depending on the ritual. You can decorate the altar with items

Orienting Your Altar

•••••◆◆◆◆◆◆◆◆••••

While orienting your altar to face north or east is traditional, each of the directions symbolizes a different purpose. Choose which one best suits you. If you don't know which direction your home or garden faces, use a compass to find out.

East: Creativity and new beginnings
South: Action and manifestation
West: Emotion and the subconscious
North: Wisdom

that have meaning to you, such as candles that have a special association, or something symbolic to the elemental power that you wish to invoke.

Below are tools you can put on your altar in order of where they generally go. You can use all of the items in the list if you like or keep things simple and use only a few. This is entirely up to you and the way you feel.

LEFT SIDE OF THE ALTAR
This is where you place the items sacred to the goddess: goddess candle, goddess statue, chalice, water bowl, aspergillum (used to sprinkle water), bell, wand, broom, and any other item associated with the goddess.

CENTER OF THE ALTAR
Censer or incense burner, cauldron, red candle, small dish for offerings to the deities.

RIGHT SIDE OF THE ALTAR
This is where you place items sacred to the god: god candle, god statue, salt bowl, pentacle, athame, bolline, matches, small plate used for cakes.

ANYWHERE ON THE ALTAR
Book of shadows, pen, herbs, oils, crystals, flowers.

✳ ✳ ✳

5

SETTING UP A SACRED SPACE

W hen witches work, they often create a space that is safe and sacred around their altar so that they can carry out their rituals and spells with no negativity to bother them. This is done through creating a circle, cleansing it, and then calling the quarters. This is good to do when you are just starting out, but you may find later you don't need to go to the trouble of doing this every time you want to perform a ritual.

Creating a Circle

Making a circle around your altar will demarcate the boundaries of your safe space. You can use stones or crystals to mark out the circle. If your altar is on a table in the middle of a room or if you set one up outdoors, you can put a large circle around it that you can walk around. Ensure there is enough room for you to sit, stand, and to move around inside the circle. If you have to use a sideboard or a kitchen counter, you can put a few ribbons, stones, or crystals around the back and sides of the altar to create a kind of half circle. Do the bits that you can manage, because the intention will be useful, even if you can't complete the entire ritual.

Once you've created the circle, burn incense, light your chosen goddess and god candles, and if you wish, put on some calming, relaxing music.

Cleansing the Circle

You can cleanse your circle when you first set up your altar as well as before you practice a spell or ritual. Walk around the edge of your proposed area in a clockwise direction starting in the east, which represents the element air. (South is linked to fire, west to water, and north to earth.) As you walk from one point to the next, ring the bell a couple of times to clear any negative

energy. This will cleanse the area that you will use for your circle, in which you will have your altar. As you walk, say the following aloud:

> *I call to the element of earth; may all negative energies leave and only*
> *positive remain.*
> *This is my will, so mote it be.*
> *I call to the element of air; may all negative energies leave and only*
> *positive remain.*
> *This is my will, so mote it be.*
> *I call to the element of fire; may all negative energies leave and only*
> *positive remain.*
> *This is my will, so mote it be.*
> *I call to the element of water; may all negative energies leave and only*
> *positive remain.*
> *This is my will, so mote it be.*

Casting a Protective Circle

After your circle is cleansed, if you wish, you can perform this ritual to protect it from negativity. Walk around your circle clockwise with incense and a feather to represent fire and air. If you can't walk around the altar, wave some incense around the sides and back of it.

Pour a little salt and water together and walk around the circle with the salted water to represent the water and earth. If you can't walk around the altar, pass this around the altar as best you can and then put the dish down again.

With the athame, wand, or even your finger, cast the circle around the altar. Make the connection with spirit using your energy and heart. Visualize a white light coming down and flooding over you and over the altar while as you walk the circle or pass your athame, wand, or finger around the altar. This will bring spirit and the strength of the universe down for you to tap into. Now sit and face your altar, close your eyes, and take a few deep breaths to calm and relax yourself.

The Protective Circle Chant

Recite, "May my circle be cast in love and trust. So mote it be."

Now call in your chosen goddess and god to join you in your circle, to watch over you, and keep you safe.

Recite, "Mother Goddess, please hear my call, come join me and watch over this circle. Father of the Sky, please hear my call, come join me and watch over this circle, and make us one."

Call in the Quarters

Once you feel your circle is cleansed and protected, you can call in the quarters to bring in help from the elements and guardians for your spells and rituals. To do this, stand at each of the four points of the compass and face outward, raise your arms, and imagine that you are calling the elements to help you. I start in the east, but you can start at whichever point feels right to you.

Now recite the following:

Hail unto you, O guardian of the east, power of air and intellect.
I ask that you guard me with the power of the sudden storm and keep
  me safe.
I ask that you be with me in my circle and aid my magic rituals.
I bid you hail and welcome!
Hail unto you, O guardian of the south, power of fire and manifestation.
I ask that you guard me with the power of the roaring flame and the softly
  fading ember.
I ask that you be with me in my circle and aid my magic rituals.
I bid you hail and welcome!
Hail unto you, O guardian of the west, power of water and emotion.

*I ask that you guard me with the power of the ocean and hold me safe like
the sacred mother's womb. I ask that you be with me in my circle and aid
my magic rituals.*
I bid you hail and welcome!
Hail unto you, O guardian of the north, power of earth and integration.
*I ask that you guard me with the strength of the land, and like the soil that
nurtures the smallest seed, I ask that you help me in my circle and aid my
magic rituals.*
I bid you hail and welcome!

Turn and face your altar, raise your hands, and say:

*Beloved Lord and Lady, I call to you join me as we meet in sacred space
and ask that you help and guide me with wisdom and love. Welcome and
blessed be.*

Now that you have cleansed and protected your sacred space and called the
quarters to ask for help in your magical rituals, when you are ready, you can
meditate, cast a spell, or just sit for a few minutes. When you have finished, you
can close down your sacred space by thanking each of the guardians in turn and
asking them to close the space. First recite, "O guardian of the east, please close
down this sacred space. Thank you." Then repeat those lines for south, west,
and north.

You must also remember that when you have completed your ritual you
will need to ground yourself. You can do this by sitting on the ground with
your bare feet touching the earth, or if it is too cold, or you are indoors,
imagine roots going down from your feet into the ground. I suggest that you
have something small to eat and a hot drink, as this will also ground you after
your work.

❋ ❋ ❋

6

THE WHEEL
OF THE
YEAR

The wheel of the year is the annual calendar of festivals celebrated by Wiccans and pagans. The festivals of the wheel of the year represent the active and dormant states of nature, humankind, and agriculture. Each of the festival days is ruled by a governing god or goddess.

The Sabbats

The eight festivals are known as sabbats. The sabbats are divided into the Greater Sabbats, which are feminine, lunar in character, and dedicated to the goddess, and the Lesser Sabbats, which are masculine, solar-based, and celebrate the god. The Lesser Sabbats also mark the equinoxes and solstices. As such, the day the sabbats fall on can change from year to year.

The Lesser Sabbats, or solar festivals, mark each seasonal change, while Greater Sabbats, or fire festivals, are usually celebrated as significant agricultural festivals. Together the solar festivals and the fire festivals make up the wheel of the year.

The Esbats

While sabbats are held as celebrations, the esbats are the magical working days and nights. These are special times when energy is sent out for special purposes, such as healing, success for a positive project, personal growth, getting rid of negativity, or ridding oneself of bad habits.

The esbats are usually celebrated at the full moon each month. Although the goddess and god are present in both the sabbats and esbats, it is generally felt that the sabbats are held in honor of the god and the course of the sun, and the esbats are held in honor of the goddess and the phases of the moon.

Timing of Festivals

These ancient festivals have their roots in the seasons as they are known in the UK and the more northerly countries of Europe. If you live in a completely different climatic area or in the southern hemisphere, you may have to adapt the seasons and the farming calendar to suit the part of the world in which you live.

The Greater Sabbat Fire Festivals	
Samhain	October 31
Imbolc	February 1
Beltane	May 1
Lammas	August 1
The Lesser Sabbat Fire Festivals	
Yule	December 21–22
Ostara	March 21–22
Lithia	June 21–22
Mabon	September 21–22

The Sabbats of the Year

Samhain: October 31

Samhain (pronounced sow-en or sow-een) is
one of our four Greater Sabbats. It is a *cross
quarter day*, situated between the autumn
equinox and the winter solstice. While the
word is Gaelic, and it means "summer's
end," Samhain is the New Year for Wiccans,
as well as the third and final harvest festival.
(The ancient Celtic year is divided into four
major quarters known as Samhain, Imbolc,

Beltane, and Lammas.) It is also known as Winter Nights or Halloween. It
marks the last opportunity to dry herbs for winter storage. This is also the
Festival of the Dead and the night when we remember and honor our departed
loved ones and ancestors. At this time of year, the veil between the world of the
dead and the world of the living is at its thinnest, and the spirits of loved ones
are thought to have the energy needed to visit us.

Samhain is a good time for personal reflection, for recognizing our faults
and flaws, and for creating a way of rectifying them. This is the most powerful
night of the year in which to perform divination; therefore many spiritual
people seek to look into the year ahead and see whether the answers appear
good or bad.

THE ALTAR FOR SAMHAIN

Decorate your altar with photographs of dead loved ones, pumpkin lanterns,
oak leaves, apples, nuts, and sage. Incenses associated with this festival include
nutmeg, mint, and sage, and candles should be colored black and orange. Place
food items on your altar, such as apples, cake, or mead, along with flowers such
as marigolds and chrysanthemums, or frankly anything you can find growing
at this time of the year. Write on a piece of paper an aspect of your life that you
wish to be rid of, such as anger, a bad habit, misplaced feelings, or sickness, and
place the paper in your cauldron. Once you have arranged your altar, light the
candles and the censer, and cast your circle.

INVOKE THE GODDESS

Light a fire within the cauldron or light a candle and put it into the cauldron, sit before it, holding the piece of paper, gaze at its flames, and say the following:

> *To all crone goddesses,*
> *I create this fire to transform all that which is plaguing me*
> *May the energies be reversed from darkness to light*

Now set fire to the paper and drop it in the cauldron's flames, and as it burns, release any pain and sense of loss you may feel and let it seep away into the cauldron's flames.

Honor the dead with your memories, but do not call them to you; leave them in peace. Many Wiccans do attempt to communicate with their deceased ancestors and friends at this time, but you should only do this if you are an experienced medium, because you may have a problem with the energies at this time of the year. Samhain is one of the most potent nights of the year for divination, candle magic, astral projection, past-life work, black mirror scrying, spells, runes, casting protection, inner work, clearing obstacles, inspiration, and transformation. It is an ideal time to read the tarot cards using a Wheel of the Year spread to forecast the year ahead.

Many years ago, bonfires were lit to protect the family, coven, or land through the winter darkness, and torches were set ablaze to honor the dead. Now we burn incense and put a candle in the window to help the spirit of a loved one find its way home. You can put a lighted candle on your altar, or place lanterns outdoors to guide the way for spirits.

Please take care when using candles not to set anything alight, and don't leave candles alone where they might set fire to a curtain or anything else.

Time for Divination

If you wish, you may attempt scrying (crystal, black mirror, or flame gazing) or some other form of divination, for this is a perfect time to look into the past and the future. You can try to recall past lives as well.

Wheel of the Year

••••◆◆◆◆◆◆••••

A Wheel of the Year tarot spread is easy to do, as all you do is lay twelve cards in a circle, with each card representing one month of the year. You can do this in a little more depth by putting three cards in each position.

Some families set a place for a missed love one at the dinner table, but if this is not for you, just sit quietly and think of those friends and loved ones who have passed away. This is a good night for deep reflection, inner work, and meditation, in which you can focus on changes, transitions, endings, and new beginnings. Release bad habits and toxic relationships, illness, failure, and poverty; in short, release everything you do not want to carry into the New Year. Sweep negativity out of your home, bring quarrels to an end, settle debts, and make amends if needed.

Samhain correspondences: black cat, bat, ghost, scarecrow, waning moon, pumpkin, apple, grain, pomegranate, mugwort, rosemary, wormwood, acorn, oak leaf, and root vegetables.

Goddesses: Crone, the triple crone goddesses, Cerridwen, Hecate, and Morrigan.

Gods: Osiris, the Horned God, Herne the Hunter, and Odin.

Incense: sandalwood, sweetgrass, and wormwood, which will help you to see the spirits of the returning dead.

Candles: new candles for the New Year are black, orange, or autumn colors. If you want to honor the Lord of the Old Year, use black candles, and if you wish to honor the Lady of the New Year, use white candles.

Tools: a besom (a twig brush or broomstick) to sweep out the old year and any negativity it contained. A cauldron, for transformation. Crystals such as obsidian, carnelian, smoky quartz, jet, and bloodstone.

Altar decorations: autumn leaves, fall flowers, pomegranates, apples, pumpkins, ears of corn, sprays of grain, corn dollies, gourds, nuts, seeds, acorns, chestnuts, and images of ancestors are all appropriate. Use whatever is in season in the place where you live, and use whatever feels right and looks good to you.

Food: gingerbread, freshly roasted nuts, nut breads, anything made with apples or pumpkin, meat (especially bacon), doughnuts, popcorn, cakes with lucky tokens in them, and red foods, because the ancients held them sacred to the dead. Drink mead, apple cider, mulled cider, and mulled wine. If you don't want to drink alcohol, make some fruit tea and drink that.

Dress: masks and costumes

Also: bobbing for apples, roasting nuts, popping popcorn, enjoying harvest feasts, any rituals that honor the dead, trick-or-treat feasts, and parties.

Yule: December 21–22

Yule is a lesser sabbat solar festival that marks the winter solstice and the rebirth of the sun. This is an important turning point because it marks the shortest day, after which the light will gradually start to increase until the summer solstice. It is the Wiccan and pagan celebration of Christmas, but the solstice doesn't always fall on the same day—the date varies from one year to the next. It marks the high point of winter and celebrates the rebirth of the sun god as Yule.

THE ALTAR FOR YULE

Put candles and festive decorations, including evergreens if you have the space for them, on your altar. Include fruit and nuts, especially walnuts, pecans, and hazelnuts, or fresh fruit such as oranges and apples.

YULE EVERGREENS

Mistletoe is a plant that grows on various trees, particularly the apple tree. It is one of the most important Wiccan herbs, as it brings romance, love, and fertility. It can help you to perceive the world beyond this one, overcome difficulties, improve health, and find what you need or what you are looking for. The mistletoe is cut using a golden sickle on the sixth day of the moon. It is associated with thunder, and regarded as a protection against fire and lighting. It is interesting to note that mistletoe was excluded from church decorations, probably due to its connection with the druids and its pagan and magical associations. (For more on mistletoe, see page 98.)

Holly is known as an evergreen of protection, and it's said that holly's spiky bristles repel unwanted spirits. Newborn babies used to be sprinkled with "holly water," made from water in which holly had been soaked and left under a full moon overnight. This evergreen is sacred to Holle, the ancient Germanic goddess of the underworld, who symbolizes everlasting life, goodwill, and life energy.

Ivy is an evergreen symbol of immortality and resurrection. It is sacred to the Egyptian god Osiris, who was believed to have died and been resurrected in ancient times.

Yew trees are often planted in graveyards, so they carry a deep connection with the spirit realms and the ancestors. It is sometimes used in ritual spaces. Note that yew has red berries that are very poisonous.

Pine branches will bring healing and joy to the home, and burning a little pine will purify the air or space.

It is traditional to make wreaths from different evergreens, and in days gone by, these were hung on doors or laid horizontally on tables and decorated with candles. This later became a Christian holiday tradition.

YULE CANDLES

Yule candles are often red, green, or gold, and they can sit in candlesticks on plates that are decorated with sprigs of holly or some other evergreen. The candles are lit on Christmas Eve, with its light shining on the festival supper and left to burn throughout the night. Another time for Yule candles is early Christmas morning, when they used to be left to burn throughout the day. The candle was rekindled on each successive night of the twelve-day festival, and finally extinguished on the Twelfth Night. While the candle burned, it was believed to shed a blessing on the household, and it was considered a sign of ill omen or misfortune for the candle to go out. Tradition says that it was also

Caution with Candles

It is never a good idea to leave candles unguarded, so use small tealight candles and put them in glass holders that keep the breeze off them. Even then, ignore the practices of the past: put the candles out and light new ones when you are able to keep an eye on them again.

considered unlucky to move the candle or to blow out the flame, so when it was time to extinguish it, it was done by pressing the wick with a pair of tongs.

A YULE RITUAL TO CLEANSE YOUR SPACE

To do a cleansing ritual, you will need to hold incense or a sage stick in your hand. Start at your front door and move the incense around each doorway and window while you go through each room, continuing up and down any stairs. Some people chant or recite an incantation while performing this process; you can say something like this one:

> *Yule is here, and I lovingly cleanse this place,*
> *Fresh and clean, in time and space.*
> *Sage and incense, burning free,*
> *As the warmth of the sun returns, so it shall be.*

When you have finished, open the windows and doors for a few minutes to let the smoke and any negative energy out, then you can enjoy the positive energy that comes with having a clear space.

Deities: Apollo, Freya, Frigga, Venus, and Odin

Planets: Sun and Jupiter

Sign: Leo

Element: Air

Tarot Correspondence: Tower, Knights, and Sixes

Imbolc: February 1

Imbolc (pronounced *Eeem*-bolc) is a festival of light and of the dawn. It is traditional to light many candles to encourage the sun to shine more brightly and for the earth to throw off the cold winter months. For this reason, Imbolc is also known as Candlemas, the Feast of Torches, the Feast of Pan, the Snowdrop Festival, Brigid's Day, and probably by many other names. It is another of the four Greater Sabbat fire festivals, and this one celebrates the first signs of spring, the first sprouting leaves and the crocus flowers. It is the festival celebrating the passing of winter and the start of the agricultural year, also the transition of the Triple Goddess from the form of the crone to that of the maiden.

Imbolc is the day on which we honor the rebirth of the sun and the Celtic goddess Brigid. She is the goddess of poetry, healing, and midwifery. She is also known as a Triple Goddess, so we honor her in all her aspects. It is a festival of light and of fertility that was once marked in Europe with huge blazes, torches, and fires in every form. These days, Wiccans light white candles for Brigid and yellow or red for other gods. The candles symbolize the start of spring and the return of the sun. It's traditional to turn on a light in every room of the house after sunset, even if it's only for a few moments. This is a good time for initiations, whether they be self-initiations or initiations into covens.

THE ALTAR FOR IMBOLC

Incenses for Imbolc are rosemary, frankincense, myrrh, and cinnamon; then add corn dollies, a small besom (twig broom), and spring flowers. Choose white, orange, and red candles, and garnet, ruby, bloodstone, onyx, or amethyst crystals. Other items might include white flowers, unlit orange candles that have been anointed with cinnamon, frankincense, or rosemary oil, or a red candle that represents the element of fire. Also, a scrap of white cloth in a small crystal bowl represents snow.

Once you have laid out your altar, light the candles and censer, mark out your circle, and evoke the goddess and the god using the following words:

It is the time of the feast of torches,
Every lamp blazes and shines to welcome the rebirth of the god.
I celebrate and welcome the goddess and the god.
So mote it be.

Light the orange or the red candle on the altar. Slowly walk around the altar clockwise, holding the candle before you. Say these words:

All the land is wrapped in winter.
The air is chilled, and frost covers the earth.
But lord of the sun, unseen you have been reborn,
Of our mother goddess the lady of all fertility
Hail great god and welcome.
And shall it be.

Ostara: March 21–22

Ostara, a Lesser Sabbat solar festival, marks the spring
equinox, when day and night are of equal length. It
is the second of the spring festivals, and it focuses on
fertility because this is the time when seeds are blessed
for planting. It is considered to be the high point of
the spring season, when life is bursting forward in all
directions. The name Ostara is thought to originate from
the Germanic word for "east," but it might also be an
early name for Easter, as Ostara was a pagan holiday that preceded the Christian
Easter. The idea of painted eggs harks back to pagan times with its images of
fertility, but Wiccans also like to bring flowers into the house at this time.

You can use Ostara to free yourself from things that hinder your progress,
so it is a good time to perform spells that help you banish bad habits or negative
thoughts and emotions. It is also a good time to perform spells that help you
regain things you have lost, or those that will help you develop qualities and
talents that you would love to have.

THE ALTAR FOR OSTARA

Decorations can be a yellow disk or wheel that you can make out of a piece of
colored card, colored eggs, or decorations in the shape of hares. Candles can
be bright or lemon yellow, light green, and pale pink. Choose incenses from
frankincense to welcome spring and to refresh your life, or jasmine or rose. Flowers
should be laid on the altar, placed around the circle that surrounds the altar, and
strewn on the ground. A small potted plant should be placed on the altar.

The cauldron can be filled with spring water and flowers, while you can
wear buds and blossoms. When you have arranged everything, light the candles
and incense, and cast the circle. Invoke the goddess and god. Stand before the
altar and gaze upon the potted plant, then touch the plant and connect with its
energies, and through it, to all nature.

Still touching the plant, you can say the following words:

> *I walk the earth in friendship,*
> *Mother Goddess and Father God,*
> *instill within me through this plant warmth for all living things.*
> *Teach me to love the earth and all its treasures.*
> *So mote it be.*

Take time to meditate upon the changing of the season, perform spells if you wish, or celebrate with a simple feast. If you wish to burn essential oils to welcome spring and refresh your life, use frankincense, orange, jasmine, rose, or other sweet or zesty oils.

Beltane: May 1

May Eve is a Greater Sabbat fire festival that is also known as the Celtic May Day. It officially begins as the moon rises on May Day Eve, and it marks the beginning of the third quarter.

Beltane is one of the major sabbats of the Wiccan religion, and it celebrates sexuality, life, and unity. It celebrates the union of the goddess and god, and, therefore, fertility, birth, and new beginnings. This is the season for love, wedding vows, ceremonies, and commitment, so it is a popular time for handfasting, which is a pagan marriage ceremony. Wiccans still perform handfastings, and they still love to do so at this time of fertility and growth. Other traditions include braiding one's hair, maypole dancing, and jumping over a small Beltane bonfire for luck.

In ancient times, rituals were performed to promote fertility, and cattle were driven between two fires to protect them from any illnesses. Druid rituals became absorbed into Christian ones, and these outdoor services were later held in churches, followed by a procession to the fields or hills, where the priest kindled the fire.

People hung rowan branches over their fireplaces in their houses on May Day to bring luck to the house. The flowers and greenery symbolize the goddess, and the maypole (a phallic symbol, of course) represents the god. Another common focal point of the Beltane rituals is the cauldron, which is also associated with the goddess. The Welsh goddess Creiddylad is often connected with Beltane, and she is also called the May Queen, the goddess of summer flowers and love. May Day has long been marked with feasts and rituals, maypoles, and dancing. People rose at dawn to gather flowers and green branches, using them to decorate the village maypoles. The May Queen and King were usually young people who would go singing from door to door throughout the town carrying flowers for the May tree and asking for donations.

Cordelia is another goddess worshipped at this time; she is known as being part of fairy realms and as a flower princess who helps with celebration. She is linked to gardening, but also to joy, and rituals to Cordelia are helpful for those going through life changes, or who need to manage increased levels of stress and need courage. One of the ways to draw Cordelia and the fairies into your life is to take a little chair from a doll's house and glue any or all the following items around it: thyme, straw, primrose, oak leaves, ash leaves, and hawthorn berries or leaves. Leave the doll's chair on a sunny windowsill, preferably one with a plant on it to encourage fairy guests who will bring all manner of spring frolic into your home.

Put fruits, flowers, and baskets around the altar and as decoration around your home. Put baskets by your front door that you have decorated with ribbons, and fill them with citrus fruits and spring flowers, as this will help guide the fairy folk to you.

THE ALTAR FOR BELTANE

Red and white are the perfect colors for a Beltane altar. Red symbolizes sexual energy, and white symbolizes purity, so maybe use a red altar cloth and lots of white flowers and buds. You can decorate the altar with a miniature maypole, flowers, and ribbons, and put your wand on the altar as well. You can use lilac and frankincense incenses. Place some ribbons in green, red, and white, or summery colors, such as greens or sky blue, on the altar, and choose herbs such as agrimony, St. John's wort, frankincense, hawthorn, ivy, marigold, or meadowsweet. If you wish, you can add orchid root, rose, rowan, woodruff, elder flowers, primroses, or rose petals. Candle colors can be light blue for tranquility and health, red for the god, and yellow for the goddess.

A beautiful addition to the altar is a bowl or cauldron of water with small tealight candles floating on the surface with flower petals, as this will make a beautiful focal point for an evening ritual, or for spell casting and magic. This is a great time to cast spells for love, romance, fertility, relationships, crops and gardening, creativity, wealth, and prosperity. I like to set up an outdoor altar in front of a tree with low-hanging branches, and I make floral chains and wreaths and hang beribboned herbal sachets on the tree for decoration.

Traditional foods for Beltane include strawberries, melons, and cherries, dairy products such as yogurts and dips, or cold soups, salads, and raw vegetable platters. The best way to celebrate is with a picnic, so pack foods like salad, coleslaw, and potato salad. Another tradition is to eat oatcakes, as these are perfect for a meal of cakes and ale. You might like to add dandelion or fruit wine or make a rich punch full of mixed crushed fruits.

Women traditionally wear colorful dresses and skirts, with ribbons and flowers in their hair and floral wreaths on their heads. Men put on capes and vests or waistcoats. Many wear vine wreaths or Green Man masks, while some even dress up like forest animals, invoking a hint of ancient shamanism.

Candle magic is highly effective at this time, as it works with the element of fire, which brings swift action. All you need is a candle in the color of your choice, some essential oil that corresponds with your goal (see chapter 10), a sharp pin or knife, and a lighter or matches. With the knife or pin carve your name into one side of the candle and your goal into the other. Take a couple of drops of the oil and rub it onto the candle, concentrating on achieving your desired outcome, then light the candle and gaze on the flame as you visualize success. Spend a few minutes doing this, and when you are ready, snuff it out with pincers. You can relight the candle every day for at least seven days, each time rubbing a little more oil into the candle to keep charging it up! You should see the results of your spell within seven days.

Lithia: June 21–22

This is the Lesser Sabbat solar festival that occurs at the summer solstice, also known as midsummer, or the gathering day. This solar festival is the most powerful day of the year for the sun god because this sabbat glorifies the sun. After this day, the sun starts to grow weaker and the days grow shorter. Fire plays a prominent role in this festival because it is seen as the element of transformation. It can burn, consume,  cook, shed light, or purify, and it is still common to light and use bonfires during midsummer rites. (Bonfires were originally signal fires or beacons, but they are now an accepted part of witchcraft rituals.)

Cultures of many kinds have marked midsummer in rituals, and people have long since acknowledged the rising of the sun on this special day. The heel-stone at Stonehenge marks the midsummer sunrise as seen from the center of the stone circle. In ancient times, the summer solstice was often marked with torchlight processions, by flaming tar barrels or wheels bound with straw that were set alight and rolled down steep hillsides, in the hope of bringing fertility to crops and livestock, and prosperity to people. Blazing Irish wildfires of gorse, also known as furze, were taken around cattle to prevent disease and misfortune, while people danced around the balefires or leaped through the flames as a purifying or strengthening rite.

Astronomically, Lithia is the longest day of the year, and from this point onward we enter the waning year. Each day the sun will recede from the skies a little earlier until Yule.

A candle should be lit for the entire day, especially if it is cloudy or raining. The fire represents the sun and is a constant reminder of the power of the god. Rituals should be performed at noon or when the sun is highest in the sky.

Some witches choose to bury their protective amulets each midsummer's eve and construct new ones for the next year. Amulets can include rue, rowan, and basil, tied together in a white or gold cloth, as this makes a protection amulet that can be carried in your pocket all year round. This is also an excellent time to renew wedding vows.

THE ALTAR FOR LITHIA

Decorations can include dried herbs, potpourri, seashells, summer flowers, and fruits. Colored ribbons can include blue, green, and yellow. You can use these incenses: sage, mint, basil, St. John's Wort, sunflower, lavender, rowan, oak, and fir.

Activities or divination are related to romance and love, so you can light a white candle in front of a mirror, recite your own wish, and allow the candle to burn out. You could float paper boats with blessings written on them on a stream to bring luck and love to whomever may find them, or to the land itself.

This festival includes singing and dancing around a bonfire, picnic feasts, and happiness. You can create a crown of flowers to wear in your hair or to place on your altar in honor of your favorite goddess.

Lammas: August 1

Lammas is also known as Lughnasa or Lugnasad, and
it is a Greater Sabbat fire festival celebrating the first
fruits of harvest, the fruits of our labors, and seeing
the wishes that we had at the start of the year unfold.
It is when Wiccans give thanks for the fertility of the
fields and the first harvest, and it comes from an early
Christian festival, with the name "Lammas" meaning
"loaf mass," as it represented the first loaves baked
from that year's cereal crop. There are many harvest festival traditions and
customs all over the world today, but in the old days, it was a time for bread
making and corn dollies with straw.

Goddesses celebrated around this time include the one known to the Greeks
as Demeter and to the Romans as Ceres. The trees associated with this sabbat
are the hazel and gorse, and herbs are sage and meadowsweet. Colors are golds,
yellows, and orange for the god and red for the goddess.

Appropriate activities include walking through the woods to spend some
time meditating in beautiful surroundings or staying at home and making
bread. It is also traditional to make a wicker doll called a wicker man, in which
you put all the bad habits or things that hold you back or any emotion you want
to be rid of, and then throw him onto the fire.

THE ALTAR FOR LAMMAS

You can make a corn doll and place a few cereal grains on an offering plate.
You can place some berries alongside the grains, but if you are to keep the altar
going for several days, be aware that at some point the berries will start to rot,
so be prepared to replace them. Alternatively, you can just use your altar for the
night and day of the festival, and then give the leftover offerings to any animals
that would appreciate them.

You can place candles on the altar, especially for Lugh, the Irish god who
is said to have created the festival. I would choose Demeter for the goddess, as
she is the goddess of nature, and she is closely tied to agriculture and grain. She
also has a sacred serpent that protected the grain from rodents. Colors to be
used on your altar should be autumnal colors, such as orange, red, brown, tan,
and yellow to represent cereal. You can use ribbons of these colors to decorate
your altar.

Other symbols of Lammas are grapes, wine, ears of corn, cornflowers or poppies, straw braids, and onion garlands. Put a candle on your altar to represent the Harvest Mother, and choose a ribbon in orange, red, or yellow. You will also need a few stalks of wheat, an unsliced loaf of bread, and a goblet of wine.

You can cast a circle, light the candle, and say:

The Wheel of the Year has turned once more,
And the harvest is coming soon.
We have enough food on our tables, and the soil is fertile.
Nature's bounty, the gifts from the earth,
gives us many reasons to be thankful.
So be it.

THINGS TO THINK ABOUT AT LAMMAS

Consider your hopes and wishes for the future and ponder the plans that you are making. Are there any sacrifices you should be making in the present that will bring benefit in the future? Scatter a few grains on the altar and say:

The power of the Harvest is within me.
As the seed falls, I too grow as the seasons change.
As the grain takes root in the fertile soil,
I too will find my roots and grow and bloom.
So shall it be.

Tear off a piece of the bread and say:

As the grain transforms to bread,
and brings us life through the winter.
I am thankful for the gift of the harvest.
So mote it be.

Eat the bread and drink some wine, then take a moment to meditate on this cycle of rebirth and how it applies to your own life, physically, emotionally, spiritually. End the ritual when the time feels right for you.

Mabon: September 21–22

Mabon (pronounced Mah-bon) is a Lesser Sabbat solar festival. It is on the autumnal equinox, when day and night are the same length, a time when nature is in balance. It is the middle of harvest and the fall season, when we start to head toward winter. Now is a time to reap what you have sown, and it is time to clear up old projects and plan the crops or plant the seeds for new enterprises, or look for a change in lifestyle. This is the time to look back on your life and to plan for the future. Warm autumn days are followed by chilly nights, and the old sun god starts to leave the earth. We have to remember that all things must come to an end, just as the sun god travels into the lands of winter. We thank those who have helped us along our way.

THE ALTAR FOR MABON

Decorate the altar with acorns, oak sprigs, pine cones, fruit, and nuts, and place a small basket filled with dried leaves of various colors on it. Or stand before the altar and scatter them so that they fall to the ground within the circle.

Say a few words like the following:

Leaves fall, the days grow cold.
The hours of day and night are balanced.
I know that life continues.
For spring is impossible without the second harvest.
Blessings to you, god, and goddess as you journey into winter.
I have sown and reaped the fruits of my actions.
Grant me the courage, joy, and love in the coming year,
Banishing worry, misery, and hate.
So mote it be.

❋ ❋ ❋

7

MOON MAGIC AND A LITTLE ASTROLOGY

The moon is closest to us in the solar system. It is not a star or a planet but a natural satellite of Earth. The moon has a profound influence upon our emotions, so it is important to choose the right moon phase for your magic work. The astrological sign you work under is also significant, and you can find information on that later in this chapter.

Try to remember that any spells for gain, increase, or drawing things to you should be done when the moon is waxing. The waning moon is a good time when you want something to decrease or to send something or someone away. The highest energy is at the full moon, and the next highest is the new moon, as these are the most powerful times for magic work and for manifesting and starting new projects.

Phases of the Moon

The phases of the moon influence your power and efficiency when performing magic work. The moon is waxing when it grows, from the time of the new moon to the full moon. When the moon is waxing, it has the effect of drawing things toward you, so this is the time to cast spells for abundance, hopes and wishes, new projects, expansion, increasing health and well-being, new love affairs, increasing knowledge, and spirituality. Also, it is a time for planting herbs and for fertility.

The moon is waning when it moves from full to new, and this will have the effect of pulling away from you, so this is a good time for getting rid of anything you don't want or need in your life. It removes negative thoughts and removes low energy vibes from your home or work. This is the time to eliminate, separate, undo, recede, let go, lose weight, release, and to remove hostile or angry situations from your orbit.

The moon's energies are strongest when the moon is full. This is a great time to bring things to fruition, manifest goals, nurture, to express passion, to heal, and to be strong and powerful.

The new moon is the perfect time to rest and to work out how to make the things you want to happen come into being. It is the best time to prepare for new projects and to figure out how to ask others for the things you want or need from them.

Moon Scrying

This form of divination uses a bowl and some water and the light of the full moon to see visions and receive messages. You won't be the first to use the moon to tell the future, because the ancient Egyptians and the Romans did this during their religious rituals. Later, Nostradamus made notes while staring into a bowl of water by moonlight—that's what gave him his inspiration.

Instructions for Moon Scrying

1. On the day of the full moon, or possibly during a lunar eclipse, find somewhere indoors where you can open a window and see the moon, or set up your tools outside.

2. You will need a table, a dark bowl, and a jug of water to fill the bowl from; also a notepad or a journal, and peace and quiet or soft, meditative music.

3. Cast your circle with your witches' tools, or visualize protective white light coming down from the universe and surrounding you and your altar. If you work with guides and helpers, call them.

4. Prepare yourself by closing your eyes and focusing your mind on the energy around you, face the moon, and bring that energy toward you. Take some time to feel that energy. It may feel as though the energy is pulling you, and soon you will begin to recognize your connection to the lunar energies.

5. When you are ready to begin scrying, you should start to feel a sense of clarity and alertness.

6. Pour the water into the bowl from the jug and visualize the energy of the moon charging the water.

7. Now position yourself so that you can see the moon's light reflected directly into the water. Stare into the water. You are looking for patterns, symbols, or pictures. You may see images moving, or perhaps words forming.

8. Sometimes thoughts pop into your head that may not mean anything right away, but write them down in your journal. They may become significant later.

Patience with Spells

····◆◆◆◆◆◆◆◆····

It often takes one or two complete phases of the moon (that is one or two months) before the spell works, so don't get downhearted if nothing happens immediately.

9. Spend as much time as you feel comfortable with, which may be a few minutes, or even an hour. Stop when you begin to feel restless or if you're becoming distracted.

10. When you are finished, write down everything you saw, thought, and felt during your session. If some of it doesn't make sense, don't worry; allow a few days to let your unconscious mind process it. It's possible that you could receive a message that's meant for someone else, so if something doesn't apply to you, think about family or friends it might be meant for.

11. You can leave your water outside overnight to charge it to use later on your altar, or you can pour it away. Remember to ground yourself, which you can do by having a hot drink and something to light to eat.

Sacred Moon Circle

You can use this ritual to create a sacred circle and space to honor Mother Earth, the seasons, ceremonies, old traditions, and the divine feminine to bring you closer to nature and set your intentions on what you wish to manifest into your life.

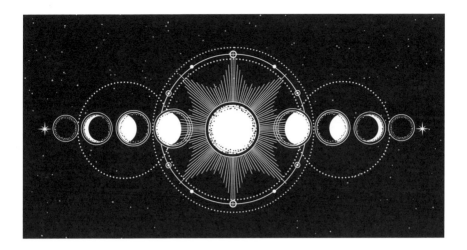

1. Choose a spot that feels good, preferably outdoors.
2. Mark off the four compass points, which are north, south, east, and west, with stones.
3. Visualize a circle that links the four compass points, then use small stones to make a smaller circle in the center. The center is your energy point.
4. Now mark out an even larger circle with stones, so that it surrounds the two inner circles. This provides a track that you can walk around, and it is also a way of keeping the energy contained. Leave a gateway for you to enter from the east and one in the west that will be your exit.
5. When forming your moon circle, you will need five stones, crystals, shells, beads, or whatever you have available. Place them at each compass point. Be mindful of how you will sit in the center of the moon circle, and place your chair or cushion so you can move about it freely.
6. Cleanse yourself and the circle by burning sage.
7. Once you have completed your circle, remember to enter from the east, and walk around your circle in a clockwise direction to bring up the energy. Three times around is usually enough, but feel free to carry on until you are happy.
8. Sit in your chair with your hands on your lap with your palms upward to begin your meditation.
9. Mentally ask your questions, and when you feel that you have your answers, give thanks to your guides, get up slowly, and leave from the west.

THE BEST DAYS
OF THE WEEK

You can also consider the days of the week when you are planning what spell to cast. Certain days are good for particular types of spells or working with different elements.

SUNDAY

Sunday corresponds to the sun, which is our closest star. You can use this day for health, happiness, success, wealth, and fame. Sundays are great for personal achievements such as working toward a promotion, seeking recognition for a job you have done well, and wealth. All these goals fall under the influence of the sun. You might do your spells sitting outside in the sunshine and calling on the goddess Brigid for illumination and inspiration. It is also the best day to cast spirit element spells.

MONDAY

Monday is associated with the moon and all her magic and mystery. Mondays are for mysteries, illusion, dream work, emotions, travel, and fertility. This day is perfect for full moon magic, so sit in view of the moon's light and absorb the energy, and call on the ancient Greek moon goddess, Selene, for practical help in magical issues. It is also good for casting water element spells.

TUESDAY

Tuesday is a Mars day, and just like the god of war, this is the time to call for strength, courage, and protection. This day of the week is for spiritual warriors. If you are facing a challenge of any kind and you need a boost to your courage, or if you want to enhance your success or to enjoy love and passion, Tuesday is the day of the week for you. It is also a good day for casting fire element spells.

WEDNESDAY

Wednesdays are linked to communication, change, study, travel, legal matters, and anything connected to the arts. This is a Mercury day, and as such, it can be a day that is full of contradictions, change, and excitement. Call upon the Greek goddess Athena, patron of arts and crafts, for inspiration for a new project. It is also a good day for casting air element spells.

THURSDAY

Thursday is a Jupiter day, so it is the day of the week for prosperity, wealth, abundance, and good health, justice, and family matters. Thursday is also the Norse god Thor's day, so it is also great for spells that help you gain strength and obtain the things you badly need. It is also a good day for casting fire element spells.

FRIDAY

Friday belongs to Venus, the planet of love, so this day is for great for all kinds of love, including self-love, birth, fertility, friendships, beauty, and romance. You can call upon the goddess Venus to help you with any romance and relationship issues. It is also a good day for casting water element spells.

SATURDAY

Saturday is associated with the planet Saturn and with karma. This is a great day for spells for protection, removing a negative situation, setting boundaries, and binding others so they can't get at you. It is a good day on which to boost your magic and spirituality, so you can call upon the goddess Hecate for guidance and protection. Saturday is also a good day for casting earth element spells.

You could use the moon sacred circle to write and perform spells, but it might not be as comfortable as doing so on an altar. If you choose to use it for spells, you need to know which direction to face.

- **North** corresponds to the element of earth, so face north for health and healing, developing your intuition, using divination, and asking for guidance from higher beings or guides.
- **South** corresponds to the element of fire, so face south for love or relationship issues, creativity, or anything of an emotional or romantic nature.
- **East** corresponds to the element of air, so face east for anything concerning your career, business ventures, financial matters, and new beginnings.
- **West** corresponds to the element of water, so face west if you need to let go of something or move on, forgive yourself or forgive someone else, or to cleanse your aura or your soul or increase your self-esteem.

A Full Moon Tea Ritual

Do you fancy the idea of doing a full moon tea ritual? This form of self-care can be used for inspiration, contemplation, and to listen to your intuition. It's a great way to create feelings of joy, peace, focus, and purpose. It involves spending a bit of time preparing and drinking tea, and you can do it alone or share it with friends and family. It is your choice, but the results will be better if

you do it by yourself. Some of you may feel emotional, with deep feelings rising to the surface during this ritual, so you'll be more at ease with them if you're alone. Frankly, it doesn't matter how you do it, as long as you do it mindfully with intention. Be conscious of how you feel and try to stay in the moment when following the ritual rather than brood about the past or consider the future. Feel free to customize the ritual to suit your own needs.

I love this tea ritual because the process of preparing it is a magical act in itself. Tea brewing involves the union of the four alchemical elements, which is why these rituals are a particularly powerful kind of magic. You don't even need a magical circle for it to work, although you can still cast one if you like, or you can set up an altar if you prefer.

Elemental correspondences:

- **Earth:** the herbs for your tea
- **Air:** the steam and scent of your tea
- **Fire:** the heat needed for tea brewing
- **Water:** the medium of your tea, in its liquid state

RECIPE FOR HERBAL TEA FOR SELF-LOVE AND SELF-ACCEPTANCE

- 1 teaspoon of rose petals
- 1 teaspoon of jasmine
- 1 teaspoon of thyme
- 1 teaspoon of lavender
- a pinch of sea salt (or table salt)
- honey for flavor
- a small teapot that makes approximately two cups
- your favorite tea set
- a mortar and pestle
- a kettle

1. Gather the petals and herbs. Using a mortar, grind each herb separately. While you're grinding them, focus on your goal. (You can substitute tea leaves or a commercial tea bag, containing herbal or fruit tea if you wish.)
2. Charge each herb one by one by drifting your fingers through them. Imagine that a white light pours out from your hands onto the herbs. When you feel the herbs tingling with energy, put them into your teapot.

3. Boil the water in your kettle. While you're waiting, prepare yourself and your sacred space, and ground yourself by planting both feet on the floor.

4. Burn some incense and light a candle.

5. When it's ready, pour the hot water onto the herbs. Focus on what you're doing, then find a place where you can see the moon. Sit near your window, or if the weather allows it, sit outside.

6. Let the tea cool down, and think about how you see yourself. Remember all the times when you've been hard on yourself. Think of the moments when you've felt that you were not good enough or not worthy of other people's love or admiration.

7. Say to yourself, "I am a good person. I am worthy of all the good things that are in my life. I am enough. I love who I am."

8. Drink your tea, and as you drink it, imagine that you're surrounded by a pink light that gives you a loving, healing, protective energy. Breathe it in, and imagine that it's filling your soul with love and compassion.

9. When there is only a small sip of tea left, stop drinking, and pour the last drop of tea into the ground as an offering.

10. Thank the moon and the universe for their help. Above all, thank yourself, because self-love is not an easy thing to achieve.

11. Pour the herbs onto the earth, and if you feel like it, write what you've felt in your journal.

The most important thing to remember is to be kind toward yourself. Self-love takes practice, and it takes time and effort if you are to achieve it.

A Little Astrology

In addition to the phase of the moon, the zodiac sign that the sun is in when you perform a spell or ritual is also important to consider. I have listed some examples of what the signs of the zodiac represent to help you to determine what to focus your magic work on during each.

- **Aries** is good for taking action and for enthusiasm.
- **Taurus** is good for renewal and sensuality.
- **Gemini** is good for anything involving communication.

- **Cancer** is good for emotion and nurturing.
- **Leo** is good for vitality and determination.
- **Virgo** is good for organizing and getting work done.
- **Libra** is good for legal matters, balance, and structure.
- **Scorpio** is good for anything that requires energy—whether this is sexual or physical.
- **Sagittarius** is good for teaching or studying, travel, and expansion of horizons.
- **Capricorn** is good for authority, ambition, and reaching goals.
- **Aquarius** is good for friendships, social occasions, and celebrations.
- **Pisces** is good for sensitivity, spiritual work, and emotions.

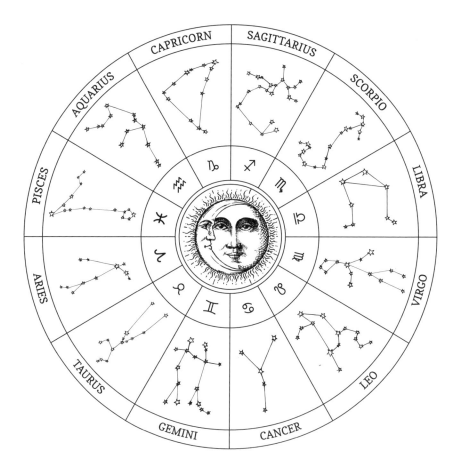

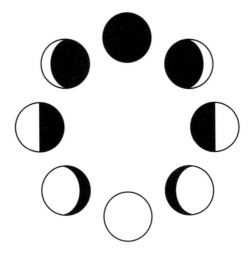

The Moon and Astrology

Each month the moon travels through all twelve of the astrological signs, but there are occasions when it is not auspicious to carry out any kind of spell casting. The first is when the moon moves from one sign to the next. This phase is called *void of course*, and it can last a day or two before it clears. You will need to put an astrology app on your cell phone or access an astrology website to know when this is happening and learn to understand the movements of the planets. Any astrologer can also tell you when this phase will occur.

Another bad time is the dark of the moon, which happens each month for a couple of days just before the new moon appears. Any magic done at these times will be a waste of time at best, or it might give you a result that you don't want.

The Planets in Retrograde

Every planet will go into retrograde motion at some point. Where the slower moving outer planets are concerned, the retrograde phase can last several months. Depending upon your own particular horoscope, this can pass by without notice, or it can mark a difficult time in your life. Witches who are adept at astrology will often check what planets are in retrograde before performing spells.

When Mercury is retrograde, it is a good time for planning, being creative, and coming up with new ideas, although it is better to put those ideas into practice once the retrograde period is over, because muddles and mishaps may occur. Fortunately, Mercury is only retrograde for about three weeks at a time.

When Venus is retrograde, matters regarding relationships slow down. If Venus is at a sensitive point in your chart, it can mark a difficult time in your love life or even with regard to friendships, especially those with women. This is not a good time to make major changes in a relationship or a friendship if you can avoid it.

Retrograde Mars makes it difficult to get anything off the ground. If this is happening in a sensitive area in your chart, it can make you angry, resentful, and really fed up. Even if Mars isn't causing you a particular problem, it is a good idea to avoid making major decisions when the planet is retrograde because your mind will lack clarity.

When Jupiter is retrograde, it is best to avoid starting a new business, going on long-distance trips, starting a course of study, or expecting others to be particularly good to you. However, it is a useful time to increase your spirituality.

When Saturn is retrograde, it's best to avoid starting a new business venture or to expect help from people in positions of authority. Father figures will let you down and most things will go very slowly; however, it is a good time to plan and negotiate.

When Uranus is retrograde, anything could happen. It is best to avoid any impulsive actions, because you may have to undo them later. However, it is a good time to work on original ideas, new inventions, or to make plans and prepare for the start of something new.

When Neptune is retrograde, it is a good time to resolve issues, but it can make it hard for anyone to think straight. Avoid escaping through drink, gambling, or drugs.

When Pluto is retrograde, you can remove and release old attachments and achieve a greater or deeper insight. However, it is not a great time for anything to do with mortgages, corporate matters, dealings with banks, borrowing money, going into any major venture, lending money to friends, or getting into anything that could lead you into a financial problem. Also avoid sexual adventures at this time because they will end up causing you more trouble than you need.

When the dwarf planet Chiron is retrograde, don't get involved in dangerous sports or activities and avoid physical fights, or you will end up with an injury. You could experience bad health at this time, so keep warm, don't take on too much, and wait for better times ahead. Interestingly, this is a good time to enjoy music, so go to a pop concert or download some great music.

❋ ❋ ❋

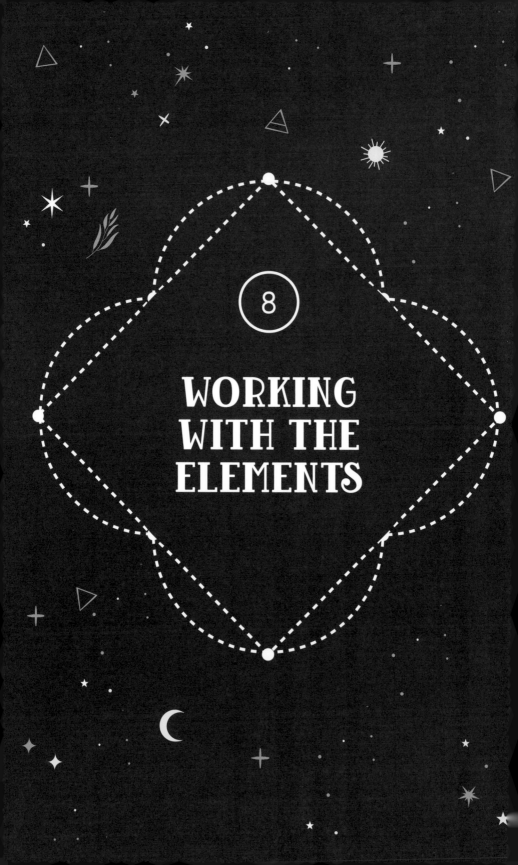

8

WORKING WITH THE ELEMENTS

Witches often use five elements when doing ritual work: earth, air, fire, water, and spirit.

The Earth Element

The Earth element represents abundance, prosperity, and wealth. It is a creative and practical element that is seen as stable and dependable. Earth sustains life and is the element on which all the other elements rest.

The earth element rules the body, growth, money, creativity, birth, death, material gain, fertility, healing, rocks, trees, animals, manifestation, materialization, crystals, silence, metal, empathy, grounding, success, strength, wisdom, and mystery.

The goddess and god that are best for this element are Cerridwen and Cernunnos.

Key associations with the earth element include these:
- The best day of the week for earth rituals is Saturday.
- The direction is north.
- The associated zodiac signs are Capricorn, Taurus, and Virgo.
- The main color is green, but others are black, brown, gold, and white.
- The season is winter.
- The best time for rituals is night, specifically midnight.
- The tools that are used with the earth element for magic purposes are the pentacle, salt, images, stones, and cord magic.
- The best crystals to use are emerald, peridot, onyx, jasper, azurite, amethyst, tourmaline, and quartz.
- The metals are iron and lead.
- Some of the plants to choose from would be cedar, cypress, comfrey, honeysuckle, ivy, magnolia, patchouli, primrose, and sage.

The Air Element

The air element is associated with the mind
and setting intentions to manifest (deciding
to make something come into being). Air
is associated with creativity, and it is allied
to higher consciousness, wisdom, and
purification.

The goddesses are Aradia and Athena, and
the gods are Mercury, Hermes, and Thoth.

Key associations with the air element include these:
- The best day of the week for air rituals is Wednesday.
- The direction is east.
- The associated zodiac signs are Aquarius, Gemini, and Libra.
- This element rules intuition, knowledge, thought, wind, breath, clouds, inspiration, hearing, freedom, revealing truth, finding lost things, memory, learning the secrets of the dead, Zen meditation, new beginnings, and bright ideas.
- For magical purposes, air rules divination, concentration, prophecy, visualization, wind magic, and karma.
- The colors associated for this element are white, yellow, light blue, lavender, and gray.
- The season is spring.
- The best time of day for rituals is sunrise.
- The tools to use are athame, sword, censer, and incense.
- Some of the crystals you can choose from are aventurine, topaz, fluorite crystals, amethyst, and yellow or blue stones.
- The metals are tin and copper.
- Some of the plants are acacia, anise, benzoin, clover, dill, frankincense, lavender, lemongrass, myrrh, pine, primrose, and violet.

The Fire Element

The element of fire is associated with sexuality and passion, which can be physical or spiritual. Everything can be brought into being quickly and filled with creative energy if you use fire magic.

The goddesses are Brigid, Freya, and Vesta, and the gods are Hephaestus and Horus.

Key associations with the fire element include these:

- The best days of the week for fire rituals are Tuesday and Thursday.
- The direction is south.
- The associated zodiac signs are Aries, Leo, and Sagittarius.
- This element rules sexuality, passions, love, authority, transformation, purification, sun, blood, healing, destruction, creativity, flame, fire, protection, courage, strength, self-knowledge, loyalty, vision, illumination, and power.
- For magic you can use candles.
- The colors associated are red, gold, crimson, orange, and white.
- The season is summer.
- The best time of day for fire rituals is midday.
- The tools used are wands, candles, a dagger, burned herbs, or requests on paper.
- The crystals you can use are red jasper, bloodstone, garnet, lava, quartz crystals, ruby, carnelian, tiger's eye, and agate.
- The metals are gold and brass.
- The plants you can choose from are allspice, basil, cacti, chili peppers, cinnamon, garlic, hibiscus, juniper, lime, mustard, nettle, onion, orange, red peppers, red poppy, and thistle.

The Water Element

Water is associated with intuition and emotions and is related to fertility.

The goddesses are Aphrodite, Isis, Mari, and Kupara, and the gods are Osiris, Neptune, Poseidon, and Varuna.

Key associations with the water element include these:

- The best days of the week for water rituals are Monday and Friday.
- The best direction is west.
- The associated zodiac signs are Pisces, Cancer, and Scorpio.
- This element rules emotions, feelings, love, courage, the unconscious mind, intuition, the womb, marriage, friendship, happiness, dreams, sleep, fertility, cleansing, purification, vision quests, self-healing, sorrow, reflection, psychic ability, oceans, rivers, lakes, and rain.
- For magical purposes, water rules sea magic, snow, ice, mirror, magnet, rain, cleansing, and purification.
- The colors are blue, blue-green, green, gray, indigo, aquamarine, and white.
- The season is autumn.
- The best times of day for water rituals are twilight and dusk.
- The tools to use are chalice, cauldron, and mirrors.
- The crystals to choose from are aquamarine, amethyst, blue tourmaline, pearl, coral, blue topaz, blue fluorite, lapis lazuli, and sodalite.
- The metals are mercury, silver, and copper.
- Some of the plants to choose from are aloe, apple, catnip, chamomile, ferns, gardenia, lemon, lettuce, lilac, lily of the valley, lotus, passion-flower, rose, seaweed, thyme, valerian, water lilies, all water plants, and willow.

The Spirit Element

The spirit element is associated with initiation, transformation, growth, and knowledge.

Use your spirit guides, angels, and helpers for this element.

Key associations with the spirit element include these:

- The best day of the week for spirit rituals is Sunday.
- The direction is center.
- The metal is gold.
- The colors are gold, purple, and white.
- You can perform these rituals any time during the day.
- The tools to use are cords, as in cord magic.
- The crystals are clear quartz and Herkimer diamond.
- Some of the plants are lotus, belladonna, and henbane.
- Call upon your spirit guides, angels, and helpers.

9

COLORS AND
CANDLE MAGIC

E very color has corresponding magical significance in
Wicca as well as a unique vibration, attribute, symbolic
value, and influence when doing spell work. Here are some of
the meanings associated with each color and, following that,
how you can use them in candle magic.

● Red

Red is linked to the south, where the sunshine comes from in the northern
hemisphere, and the element of fire. It denotes strength, health, vigor, courage,
energy, vibrancy, survival, will power, and action. It is linked to career goals.
Red attracts and magnetizes, so it is concerned with lust, passion, sexual love,
and physical desire. Red is also associated with danger, enemies, and war.

● Rose

Rose is great for treating heart ailments, anxiety, and depression. It is also good
for people who suffer from nightmares.

● Pink

Pink is a mixture of red and white, so like red, it also represents a southerly
direction and a partial connection to the element of fire, although less so than
pure red. Pink is linked to femininity and the emotions, but also to honor,
service, compassion, caring, nurturing, spiritual and conventional healing,
peace, romance, affection, emotional love, family, and friendship.

● Orange

Orange is associated with encouragement, adaptability, stimulation, vitality,
energy, stamina, mental agility, attraction, kindness, fun, luck, fortune,
prosperity, plenty, success, business, career, ambition, justice, legal matters,
and taking action.

● Yellow

Yellow is linked to the east and the element of air. Yellow is associated with
the sun, activity, creativity, imagination, visualization, knowledge, learning,
concentration, confidence, insight, memory retention, persuasion, charm,
comfort, joy, and travel. It clears mood swings and depression, and helps in
overcoming mental blocks.

Green

Green is linked to the north and the element of earth. Green is associated with fertility, growth, rejuvenation, herbal healing, physical healing, tree and plant magic, employment, ambition, personal goals, prosperity, success, finances, luck, charity, and harmony. Green, though often associated with greed and jealousy, can actually help counteract them.

Emerald Green

This color attracts love and aids with fertility. It counteracts the ambition, greed, and jealousy of others, and helps you rid yourself of any of these negative emotions. In a ritual, it brings prosperity, money, wealth, and success.

Blue

Blue is linked to the west and the element of water. Blue is concerned with tranquility, peace, calm, patience, understanding, reassurance, guidance, devotion, inspiration, wisdom, creativity, sincerity, honor, loyalty, truth, health, cleansing, emotions, harmony, psychic work, meditations, astral projection, prophetic dreams, and protection during sleep.

Light Blue

Light blue is a spiritual color that helps you obtain wisdom, harmony, inner light, or peace. It brings truth and guidance, tranquility, patience, and calm.

Dark Blue

Dark blue represents laughter and joy, wisdom, self-awareness, change, peace and calm, sleep, truth, dreams, and loyalty.

Magenta

Use this color where immediate action and extreme levels of power or spiritual healing are needed.

Gray

Gray resonates with balance and neutrality. It helps when you need to cut something out of your life, or it can be useful when you need to clear away muddles and obtain clarity.

⬤ Copper

Copper is linked to passion, money goals, professional growth, and fertility in business and career moves.

⬤ Purple

Purple rules power, success, idealism, independence, ambition, wisdom, and recognition. It is strongly associated with psychic ability, protective energy, psychic manifestations, the psychic third eye, meditation, astral projection, spiritual protection, and healing.

⬤ Brown

This color is particularly connected to grounding, concentration, and telepathy. It attunes with trees and with the protection of familiars, pets, and animals. Use brown when you need to find lost objects. Brown can also help when you feel hesitant or in need of protection, friendship, and stability, or when you want to be more decisive. It also helps with financial matters.

⬤ Black

Black is one of the traditional colors of the Samhain Sabbat and the goddess in her crone aspect. It represents deep levels of the unconscious, deep meditation, and protection. It can be used when you want to rid yourself of unhelpful habits or banish evil or negativity. It helps when you need to cut away difficult people or situations, and it helps in times of loss, discord, and confusion. It is said to enable shape-shifting.

◯ White

White may be used to represent any other color, but on its own it represents spirituality, sincerity, spiritual enlightenment, truth seeking, spiritual strength, and contacting spirit helpers. It helps to balance the aura, heal, bring peace, and cleanse. It can be used in defensive magic and when one needs physical energy. White is also linked with the goddess, the higher self, consecration, meditation, divination, the full moon, and clairvoyance.

Silver

Silver connects to the Mother Goddess, the moon, purity, values, female energy, and the unconscious mind. It helps develop psychic abilities, psychometry, clairvoyance, telepathy, intuition, and dream interpretation. Silver removes negativity, and encourages stability and good communication.

Gold

Gold connects to the Father God, the sun, cosmic influences, male energy, the conscious mind, intelligence, attracting happiness, activity, winning, healing and rejuvenation, wealth, and financial wisdom.

Candle Spells

Burning candles for ritual purposes has been around for centuries, and candle spells and rituals are really easy to do. They work well as long as you believe in their efficacy. All you have to do is light the candles, close your eyes while repeating a spell or concentrating on the things that you want to happen, and visualize them coming true. Candle spells can be as easy or as complicated as you want to make them. It all depends on how much time you want to spend. It can be as simple as lighting a green candle and saying something like, "Money, money, come to me," but a candle spell can also be long and complicated and last over several days with candles being relit each day.

You can make up your own spells to suit your needs. Think of your wish, then come up with a few words to tell the universe about your desire. It doesn't even have to rhyme. Write down your spell in your book of shadows so you can use it when you like, record how it worked, and change it as need be.

To perform a candle spell, buy the appropriate color candles for your desired outcome. I find small wax candles work best. Then anoint the candle with an oil such as olive oil, which you keep for this purpose. Rub the oil onto the candle from the middle of the candle outward using your fingers, and while you do this, think about your intention or the outcome that you want to achieve. You can sit quietly and meditate on your wish after lighting the candles and then read out your spell. This is all about will, the power of positive thinking, and creative visualization, as this will send the vibrations out into the universe.

Wish Candles

ALWAYS PRACTICE FIRE SAFETY!

Only light candles when they are securely placed in holders. Do not light them near any hanging fabrics or other flammable materials. Do not light them outdoors when conditions are dry. Make sure your candles aren't left unattended and are completely out before leaving the room or space.

These types of candles are great to use whenever you or your loved ones need a little cosmic help. Just say your wish or write it down, then light your candle and send your intention out to the universe. If you are asking for something important, repeat the wish spell over three days, because Wiccans believe in the power of three. Remember that if you can't find a candle of the appropriate color, you can always use a white one.

✸ ✸ ✸

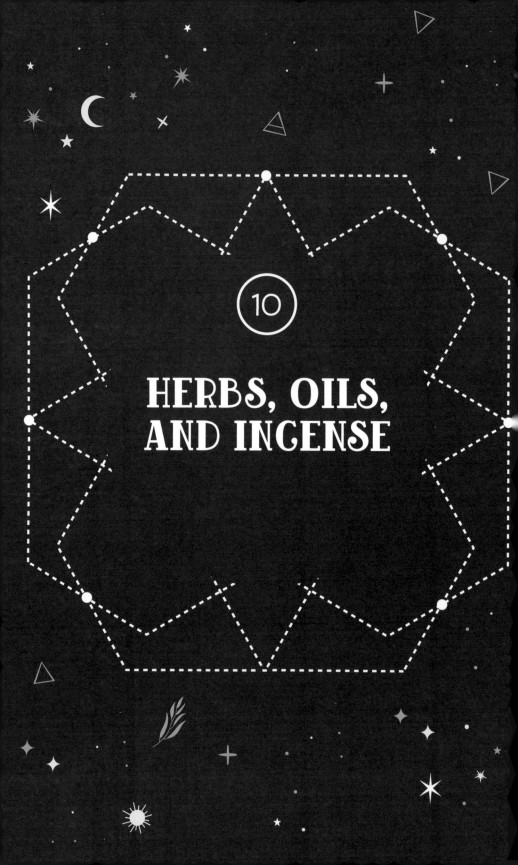

10

HERBS, OILS, AND INCENSE

M agical herbs, oils, and spiritual incense all have symbolic aspects that can enhance the results in a magical spell or ritual ceremony.

Herbs Used in Magic

Herbs are used in magic and spells for their "vibrations" or "essences." Herbs have gender, they are ruled by a planet, an element, and are often associated with a god or goddess. This is known in Wicca as the herbal correspondence, and it is an important element of Wiccan spells.

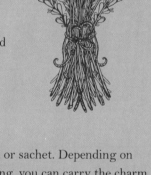

Growing and caring for herbs in your own garden can give you the advantage of putting your own energies into the plant so it becomes influenced by you rather than by other people.

In spell work, herbs can be sprinkled or placed around your home, altar, or sacred circle, or wherever you carry out your spell casting. You can also find or make a small bag in a suitable color for your purpose and fill it with herbs to make a charm or sachet. Depending on your purpose and the sort of spell you are performing, you can carry the charm with you, put it under your pillow, hang it in the house or in your car, or you can bury or burn it.

Here are some examples of how you can use herbs.

INCENSE

Herbs can be burned as ritual incense. An example is the sage smudge sticks that are used to clear negative energy and vibrations from your home or space.

BATHING

Find or make a sachet and put your desired herbs in it. Lavender can make a very relaxing bath, and you can use certain herbs to help with other conditions, such as putting eucalyptus in a bath when you have a cold or flu.

OILS

Place some herbs into a carrier oil and let them infuse for a few days, then strain and pour the infusion into a small bottle for future use as a ritual oil. Coconut or almond oil are good carrier oils for making your own beauty treatments for your hair, skin, and nails.

FOODS

Herbs such as rosemary, marjoram, basil, oregano, sage, or thyme can be used for cooking.

Using Specific Herbs

Here is a short guide to some of the herbs I find most useful.

Rosemary can be used in healing, protection, purification, stress relief, memory, and mental clarity. It is easily found in incense and essential oil form.

Lavender is good to put in little sachets and to make your own mini dream pillows (small handmade pillows you keep on your bed or under your pillow to help you sleep and have good dreams), and it can be used loose in incense or oil. It is good for protection, relaxation, improved sleep, psychic knowledge, beauty, love, and happiness.

Thyme can be made into a tea, or you can buy the essential oil. This is good for healing, purification, love, and psychic knowledge.

Sandalwood is mainly used as incense, although you can also buy it as an essential oil. It is useful to create harmony, protection, purification, and spirituality.

Frankincense is one of my favorites, as it can be burned in many forms and is good for rituals, psychic protection, healing, divination, and relaxation.

Rose is a great one for love and romance, so you can use rose oil to anoint candles, stones, love spells, and for beauty, healing, and luck.

Jasmine is known as an aphrodisiac. It can be used for love, desire, passion, emotions, dreams, and prosperity.

Patchouli is often used as incense because the oil smells lovely. It can be used for prosperity and protection, and it's also very uplifting.

Mugwort is associated with psychic awareness and is often used in scrying, divination, visions, and intuition. Don't put mugwort oil directly on the skin as it can cause a reaction.

Oils in Wicca

The use of oils goes back thousands of years. Many of the essential oils used by ancient civilizations are still available to us today, so we still make blends that re-create the traditional recipes. Let's take a look at the different types of oils used in Wicca today.

Spiritual oils are made with a blend of essential oils for a specific purpose. They can be used as aromatherapy oils, ritual oils, or essential oils (all of which we'll discuss here), and they are among the most common tools used in casting a spell. Spiritual oils are associated with the element that Wiccans call spirit, because they help us to reach out, summon, and communicate with spirit helpers in rites and rituals. Candles, crystals, amulets, talismans, and other charms may be anointed with spiritual oils, which is a great way to turn simple items into magically empowered tools.

Essential oils are concentrated oils, usually having the characteristic smell of the plant they come from. They are used to make perfumes and to accentuate ritual and spiritual oil blends. Synthetic fragrance oils are compounds that have

MAGIC AND MISTLETOE

Mistletoe stands for romance, searching for love and fertility. It is one of the most sacred pagan herbs, and it can help you to perceive the world beyond this one, overcome difficulties, improve health, and find what you need or what you are looking for. Carry or wear mistletoe for aid in conception, protection against lightning, fires, and misfortune, and burn it to banish evil. Placed at the head of the bed it gives restful sleep and beautiful dreams.

Mistletoe was sacred to pagans, witches, and druids. Branches of mistletoe were hung from ceilings to ward off evil spirits in ancient Europe. The British Celts decorated their house with holly, mistletoe, and ivy to celebrate the winter solstice, while the European mistletoe (*Viscum album*) figured prominently in Greek mythology.

Although many sources say that kissing under the mistletoe is a purely English custom, there's another story behind its origin that extends back into Norse mythology. It's the story of a loving, overprotective, mother, Frigga the goddess of love and beauty, whose son was a Norse god called Baldur. She loved her son so much that she wanted to make sure no harm would come to him. She went through the world, securing promises from the four elements of Fire, Water, Air, and Earth that they would not harm her son.

Loki, a sly, evil spirit, found the loophole she overlooked, which was mistletoe. He made an arrow from its wood. To make the prank even nastier, he took the arrow to Baldur's brother, Hodr. Hodr was blind, so Loki guided Hodr's hand and directed the arrow to Baldur's heart, killing him instantly.

Frigga's tears became the mistletoe's white berries, but eventually Baldur was restored to life. Frigga was so grateful that she reversed the reputation of the offending plant, from a symbol of death to a symbol of love, and promised to bestow a kiss upon anyone who passes under it.

Use mistletoe in spells for protection, love, hunting, fertility, health, exorcism, fidelity, immortality and also use it as an aphrodisiac. However, only do this by placing it on an altar; never eat or drink anything with mistletoe in it.

A MISTLETOE LOVE SPELL

Mistletoe is excellent to use for a love spell, and the winter is the perfect time of the year to perform such a spell. In a dish, combine mistletoe leaves with its berries, some pine needles, and a little pink glitter. Cast your magic circle and call in the four elements. Place the dish on your altar.

You will need:

- 1 spoonful of salt grains
- 1 sprig of dried mistletoe
- 1 smooth, rounded stone

To prepare:

- Grind the salt in a mortar with a pestle.
- Grind the mistletoe in the mortar.
- Rub the stone into the mixture.
- Kiss the stone.

Say these words:

> *Mistletoe, herb of love.*
> *Bring me the perfect partner.*
> *With this kiss, I share to thee.*
> *From the depths of my heart.*
> *For I wish, to find my true love.*
> *So mote it be.*

You now have a lucky love charm. Sit for a few minutes every day sending your intentions out to the universe by simply rubbing the stone. Keep it on the altar until either the next full moon or new moon, then keep it in a safe place in order to receive love and luck.

been created in a laboratory to smell like flowers or herbs. These synthetic oils are much less expensive than essential oils. For magic purposes, it's always best to use pure essential oils whenever possible, as these contain the magical properties of the plant.

Carrier oils are vegetable and mineral oils that are used to dilute the essential oils that might cause irritation or an allergic reaction if applied to the skin undiluted. Olive oil has an ancient history of being used as a carrier oil, and it is often used in oils that help in blessing and anointing. Almond oil became a popular carrier oil due to its lighter scent and texture. Unlike olive oil, it doesn't affect the natural fragrance of herbs and essential oils when blended with them.

Ritual oils, also called anointing oils, are used to anoint candles, ritual tools, and the body so that the energies of the oil can be utilized. For instance, a power oil will energize, a courage oil will give strength and bravery in the face of fears and adversaries, and a blessing oil will convey the grace of the goddess you are calling upon for help with new ventures. If, like me, you love working with pure essential oils, they can become some of your most important tools.

Condition oils is a term found only in Hoodoo and Conjure practice. It refers to all anointing and dressing oils that are used in rites, rituals, or spell casting to address or remove an unwanted condition or to bring about a desired outcome. These oils are also known as Conjure oils, Hoodoo oils, and lucky oils.

Aromatherapy oils have been used in healing techniques that can be traced back more than 6,000 years; they were used by ancient Egyptians, Greeks, Persians, Romans, and probably also the Chinese. Ancient people used to burn scented flowers and herbs or enjoy aromatic baths, massages, and beauty and cosmetic treatments using oils.

Using Caution with Oils

Before applying an oil to your body, do a patch test on a small area to make sure you don't have a reaction to it. It is always a good idea to dilute essential oils in carrier oils before applying them to your skin. Pregnant women should check with their doctor before using oils on their body or putting them in the bath. Always read the labels and, if in doubt, don't use them.

Mineral oil has one or more ingredients that are minerals. The energies of these oils come from the minerals, such as sulfur, lodestone, or pyrite, and are amplified by a carrier oil. Mineral oils have been used for blending Hoodoo condition oils.

Oils and Their Uses

Here is a list of oils and the types of spells and rituals they can be used in.

Oil	Uses
Angelica	Protection, healing, visions, removing hexes
Balm of Gilead	Love, manifestations, protection, emotional healing
Burdock	Protection, healing, happy home
Carnation	Protection, strength, healing, vitality
Celery Seeds	Passion, mental and psychic powers
Dandelion	Divination, calling spirits, favorable winds
Dill	Money, love, sexuality, protection (especially of children)
Elderberries	Prosperity, protection, sleep, banishing of negative entities
Fenugreek	Money, mental powers
Frankincense	Spirituality, protection, banishing negative entities, consecration
Gardenia	Love, peace, healing, enhancing spiritual connections

Oil	Uses
Ginseng	Love, passion, vitality, wishes, healing, beauty, protection
Hyssop	Purification, protection, prosperity
Irish Moss	Money, luck, safe travel
Jasmine	Love, money, sleep, dreams
Juniper	Protection (especially from thieves), love, health, banishing negative entities
Mugwort	Divination, clairvoyance, psychic powers, dreams, protection, strength, astral projection
Mustard	Fertility, money, protection
Nettle	Protection, healing, passion, banishing negative entities
Orris	Long-lasting love, divination, protection
Parsley	Purification, protection, passion, fertility
Passionflower	Peace, friendship, popularity, sleep
Pine	Healing, protection, fertility, money, banishing negative entities
Poppy	Fertility, love, money, luck, sleep
Raspberry	Love, protection of the home, alleviating labor pains

Incense

Incense comes in many shapes, sizes, and forms. A lot of incense comes with the herbal properties, name, and purpose clearly stated on the packaging. Don't worry too much about this, but instead buy the incense you like, because not everyone can tolerate the strength of some of the fragrances, and you could end up having to put up with a smell that you don't like.

I will list a few scents that are suitable to use for certain types of spells and rituals, but you will have to try a few to see which ones work best for you.

SPELLS FOR HEALTH
Cedar, eucalyptus, juniper, lavender, myrrh, sage, sandalwood, pine, frankincense, lemongrass, and lemon balm

SPELLS FOR LOVE
Musk, rose, chamomile, jasmine, lemongrass, patchouli, and basil

SPELLS FOR WORK
Cedar, clove, vanilla, sage, mint, wisteria, nutmeg, and honeysuckle

SPELLS FOR SPIRITUALITY, MAGIC, AND MEDITATION
Frankincense, jasmine, sage, sandalwood, rose, gardenia, and sweetgrass

For anything relating to women's issues you can use musk, rose, orange, and frankincense. For anything relating to men's issues you can use cedar, musk, jasmine, and frankincense.

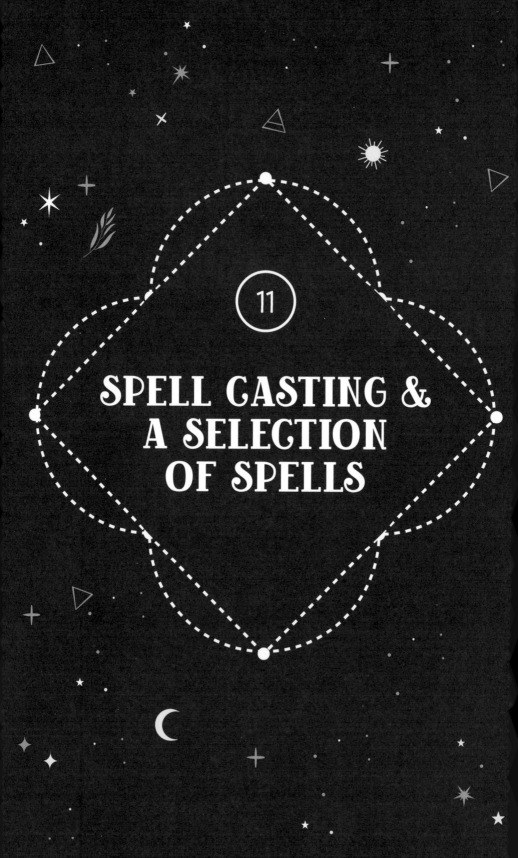

11

SPELL CASTING & A SELECTION OF SPELLS

Now that you've set up a sacred space and learned about the different symbols, tools, and materials that witches use, it's time to consider casting your own spells. You may wonder if a homemade spell can work, but you keep such spells under your own control, so they certainly will work. If you think about a spell being a bit like putting together a recipe, you will soon get the hang of it. There is no specific way of creating the perfect spell, so you should experiment until you feel happy with what you are doing. Here are a few tips to help you write your first spell.

Affirmation of Power

Before you start doing any spell work, it's often a good idea to take some time and think about the things that you value about yourself. Write down your positive attributes and the nice things people have said about you that made you feel valued and proud of yourself.

Now take a gold candle and a piece of rose quartz crystal, put the candle into a holder, light it, and then hold the rose quartz in your hand. Close your eyes and tell yourself all the positive things you have written about yourself. Add more if they come to mind. This crystal will become a token of your strength and power, so carry it with you to remind you of how wonderful you are.

THINK ABOUT YOUR PURPOSE

First, you need think about exactly what it is that you are trying to accomplish. Be specific—don't plan on doing a general spell for love, when what you actually want is to find a new love or reconnect with an old love. A specific spell is more likely to succeed.

WHAT DO YOU NEED?

Once you have worked out your intention, put the right materials together to make the spell. Use candles in colors that relate to your spell, along with herbs, crystals, oil, and a small piece of paper to write on.

WHAT TO SAY

Not all spells have to have words, but they do help you focus your energy on your intention when you are casting. This can be a hard part if you are not very creative, but just keep it simple and try to make the words rhyme, although that is not necessary.

When to Cast Spells

Pick the right day and check out the moon phases. Maybe you need a full moon to give your magic a real boost.

Now put it all together, visualize your intentions, and visualize the creation of energy around you while you focus on your task. Picture everything in your mind while you work. This can take practice, but it is where experience comes in. It's your inner thoughts and intention that make spells work.

Spells for Certain Purposes

Renew Your Spiritual Energy Spell

This spell will help to renew your spiritual self as the earth does to itself every spring.

You will need:

- A small black candle
- A small white candle
- A medium-size yellow or
  green candle
- A small spring wreath to fit around
  the candle; handmade is best
- Sandalwood incense
- Your favorite essential oil or a scent
  that reminds you of spring, diluted
  in a carrier oil, such as olive or
  almond oil
- Paper and a pen with black ink and another pen with gold ink
- A cauldron or fireproof container

Tear the paper in half, and use the black pen to write on one half sheet; title the page BE GONE. With the black pen, write down all the habits, feelings, situations, and so on that you want to get rid of. Use the back of the sheet if you need more space. Place this negative list under the holder that contains the black candle. Now leave the spell material where it is and come back to it later.

Meanwhile, take a nice cleansing bath or shower to clear yourself of any negativity. Just visualize the water washing over your body and taking all the trouble away. After the bath or shower, anoint yourself with the diluted essential oil. The wrists are a good place for this. Then dress in something white and comfortable, or carry on working sky-clad (with nothing on) if you prefer.

Return to your work space and take the other half of the paper, and with the gold pen title the page REBIRTH. With the gold pen, write all of those things you want in yourself to be better, to change the negative to the positive, and list the goals you desire to accomplish. Make positive, active statements and avoid words like *should, would, wish, hope* or anything that has half-hearted connotations. Instead, write *I will, I can* and so on. This is your positive list, so fill it with vibrant positive energy. When your list is complete, place it under the candleholder with the white candle.

Now, light the black and white candles and the incense. Take the incense holder and walk around your space three times clockwise. Take the negative list from under the black candle and use its flame to set the list alight, then quickly put it in the cauldron.

As you do this, say the following words:

What once was will never be.
I'm making room for the new me.
Be gone, be gone!
So mote it be!

After the negative list has been burned, take the positive list from under the white candle. Now here is where you need to be quick and steady. Set the positive list alight with the white candle and immediately use the burning list itself to light your yellow or green candle, then throw the burning paper in to the cauldron. If you are likely to burn yourself while doing this, use a match.

Now say the following words:

Let me feel, let me see,
Now reborn in positivity.
As I walk into spring,
Let all good things now come in.
So mote it be!

Gaze at your green candle for a few moments and meditate if you wish. When you're ready, take the cauldron outside and throw the ashes to the wind, making sure it doesn't come back into your house or your face. Make sure you pinch the candles out and throw the candle stubs away. Get something nice to eat or drink and begin to enjoy your renewed self.

A Spell for Money

There is a debate on whether it is ethical to perform money spells, but I believe there is enough universal energy to go around for all of us. I wouldn't work a spell with the intention of manifesting millions because that would just be greedy. But we all need money to live, and that is reasonable to re-quest. As an acquaintance of mine says, ask for abundance (money)  "for the need, not for the greed." You could even ask for opportunities to make more money.

Spiritual theory says that the universe will give you what you need to be comfortable. But I don't believe that, because plenty of people get into money problems that ruin their lives.

However, if you are the type of person who has been programmed to think you don't deserve to be comfortable, that will prevent you from having anything. You need to give yourself permission to receive abundance. You can do this with daily affirmations, for example, "I give myself permission to receive the abundance and prosperity that I deserve." It can also be helpful to spend a few minutes each day doing some deep breathing and imagining yourself surrounded by the things that you wish for, or what you want to use the money for. Say, for instance, if you are short for the rent payment, imagine the bill being paid and imagine the relief that you will experience. Believing it will happen helps put positive intentions out to the universe.

Take a citrine and hold it during your meditation and focus your thoughts on it afterward. Place the citrine on your altar when you cast your spell, and when you have finished, keep the crystal in your pocket so that it stays within your aura for a few days.

A SIMPLE CANDLE MONEY SPELL

You will need:

- A green candle
- A white candle
- A little olive oil

This spell may be done at any time, but aim to do it the same time each day. The green candle represents money, and the white candle represents you. Make sure you anoint the candles with oil, first thinking of your needs. Set the candles on your altar or table at each end so they are separated from each other.

Now say the following words:

Money, money come to me,
In abundance three times three,
May I be enriched in the best of ways,
Harming none on its way,
This I accept, so mote it be.
Bring me good fortune, three times three.

Repeat this spell for seven days, and each day move the white candle and the green candle nearer together, so when the candles touch each other, your spell is finished. Don't forget to visualize the money pouring in from the universe.

To Bind an Enemy

Even the nicest people can end up with an enemy. Sometimes we have enemies who do not even know us, but who dislike us out of jealousy or because they find great delight in sending all sorts of negativity our way. While you can handle a great deal of what comes your way, sometimes a binding is necessary for people who do not know when to stop. This means a kind of psychic wrapping that keeps a person from continuing to behave badly toward you. This is a simple spell on the surface, but you can make this stronger by adding other elements into the spell if you choose to do so.

You will need:
- A piece of paper
- A black ink pen
- A piece of black cord or thread
- Scissors
- A black candle
- A small glass jar
- A small iron nail

The method:
- Gather together all the items and place them on your altar or sacred space.
- If casting a circle, do so now, keeping a focus on the bully in question.
- Use the scissors to cut a length of black cord or thread about six inches long, and set it beside the jar.
- Write the name of the enemy on the paper.
- Cross their name, which means write your own name over theirs. Do this diagonally to symbolize that you are the victor in this battle.
- While doing this, imagine their energy fading before your eyes.
- You can add runic letters or any other symbols or sigils, if you think they are necessary.
- Using a trifold method, fold the paper so the names are inside, then fold it again to lock the names inside.
- Using the ribbon or thread, tie the paper so it's secure. Light the candle and drip a bit of wax over the knot and onto the paper to hold the knot in place.

Say the following:

I bind you here with my will and might
Now you cannot harm me day or night,
From your ill intentions I'll be set free,
From now on, so mote it be.

Now place the bound paper inside the small glass jar and seal it with wax around the top of the jar. You can increase the power of the binding by adding things to the jar that represent the five elements to strengthen the spell.

Elemental materials could be something like the following:
- A match to represent fire
- A little salt to represent earth
- A piece of blue paper to represent air
- A few drops of spring water
- Write the name of your spirit guide or your favorite deity on a bit of white paper to represent spirit

Try to do the spell at the right time and on the right day to help the magic. Most of us just want to distract the enemy so that they lose interest and focus, and we do not wish to harm them. Remember that curses or bad spells always come back on you threefold, so don't set out to hurt anybody. However, you are within your rights to protect yourself, and that is what this spell will do.

Banishing Spells

Banishing spells will remove someone from your life. A typical banishing spell will block or push someone away. This spell directs someone's thoughts back toward themselves, making you seem unavailable to them or even invisible to them.

You will need:
- A small mirror
- A photo or drawing of the person
- A piece of onyx
- A pinch of mugwort

The method:
- Place the mirror flat on a table and sprinkle a pinch of mugwort in one spot on the front of the mirror. Lay the photo facedown on the mirror so the face of the person is over the mugwort.

Repeat the following words:

You cannot see me,
You cannot hear me,
You do not want me,
Now leave me be.

Now set the piece of onyx on top of the photo, repeat the words again, and leave the items on your altar to keep this person away. For the most powerful effect, cast this banishing spell on the night of the new moon.

Frozen in Time Spell

Another classic banishing technique is to "freeze" someone to make them stop bothering you. This is simple spell to use to stop a person if you feel that you are getting unwanted attention that feels negative.

You will need:
- A small piece of paper
- A black ink pen
- A small piece of black string
- Water
- A fridge/freezer
- A small clear plastic or polythene bag

The method:
- On the piece of paper, write the name of the person you want to banish.
- Tie a single knot in the middle of the string, and as you tie it, concentrate on why this person is bothering you.
- Fold up the paper, with the piece of string tucked in the middle.

- Add a few drops of water to the paper. Don't soak it; otherwise you will ruin the name inside. Just dampen the paper enough that it will freeze.
- Place the wet folded paper in the plastic bag, put it in the freezer, and leave there until the situation has passed.

A Simple Spell to Help Sell a House

This spell is best done after the full moon while the moon is waning, because this energy concerns removing the obstacles to selling or letting go of your house. I start by cleaning the house from top to bottom and then doing a spiritual cleansing. We often form attachments to our home, some of which are positive and others negative, and when we can't sell a house, it may be because these attachments are holding us back from moving on with our lives.

The other thing I have noticed is that we are sometimes forced to wait until the time is right. This is an example of divine timing, which means we may have to wait until the new home that we are meant to buy is available.

You will need:
- A black candle
- A green candle

The method:
- Light a large black candle, and while doing so, ask that all obstacles be removed that keep you from selling your house and any remaining attachments be cleared.
- Light this candle for a couple of hours and then snuff it out.
- The next day, light it again for another couple of hours and snuff it out again.
- After doing the same on the third day, snuff it out for good.
- While doing all this, focus on your intention to sell.
- To speed up the selling process, you might like to write this request on a piece of paper and burn it each day before you put out the candle.

- Keep going…
- Take an image of a loved one who is in spirit (that is, who has died) and ask for their help.
- Bury the image outside your front door facing the road.
- Light a green candle.

Now say the following:

Please help bring me a sale that's quick and fair and good for me.
So be it.

Repeat the lighting of the candle and say the words for three days. You may wish to write down your intention afresh and burn the paper each day, then as you snuff out the candle, thank your loved one and all the other spiritual beings you work with for their help.

You can also say this affirmation each morning and night:

It's time to let go.

Visualize the "sold" sign on your house, and know that the right person will come along at the right time and the price will be right.

Career Spell

This spell can help you get a promotion or a new job. It can help you overcome obstacles, such as troublesome colleagues or overcompetitive clients, and move things in the right direction.

You will need:
- Cedar incense
- Cedar oil
- An orange candle
- Paper and pen
- A carnelian crystal

The method:

- Start by casting your circle and, if you wish, calling in the four quarters of north, south, east, and west. Calling the quarters entails the summoning or evocation of the watchers or spirit entities who rule over the elemental energies and reside in the direction they are called from. North is the earth element, east is the air element, south is the fire element, and west is the water element.
- Light the incense and invite your goddess to come forward to help you. In this case, you could choose to call upon either Brigid or Fortuna.
- Work the oil into the candle, starting in the middle and working outward to each end, putting your intention into the candle.
- When you are done, light the candle.
- Write the job qualities you are looking for on the paper, including anything you particularly want to happen, and a date or time limit if you think this is necessary.

Hold the crystal in your hand and say out loud:

I charge this crystal to guide me to find the right job for me,
To give me the confidence I need to work in harmony with my
future employer.

Sit quietly and visualize yourself applying for the role, going to the interview, and then being given the job. When you are done, thank the goddess for assisting you, release the quarters, and open the circle. Just let the candle burn down, and carry the crystal with you until you get your new job. Only after you have started your new position, burn the paper with your intentions on it and bury the ashes outside.

Sigil Magic

At its heart, sigil magic is where you turn your desires into reality by creating sigils (symbols) of your desires and focusing positive energy into them. The sigil then acts as a magical beacon that manifests the desire into your reality. A sigil is a sign, word, or image that is considered magical in some way. It is any image or design that has been charged with energy, and in doing so, it is

HELP, MY SPELLS AREN'T WORKING!

Here are the main reasons you may not have success in the beginning. Start by looking at your ingredients. If you feel that an herb or ingredient feels right for you and that you need to use it a certain way, then it may be a good idea to give it a try. Even if something isn't normally used in a particular spell, if it feels right for you, it is right for you. Ingredients are usually listed for a reason, because many practitioners over the years have experimented and found the energies in certain ingredients that work best for specific goals in spell crafting.

Before crafting a spell, make sure you actually *know* what your goal is and set your intent. Make sure you are really clear about what you are trying to accomplish. If you are not sure or precise and clear, this uncertainty will manifest in your spell. New practitioners tend not to have much internal power and experience because they haven't worked with magic and energy long enough to develop it, so a few failures are to be expected. I would encourage those starting out to cast quite a few smaller and less important spells. They can be for simple things like asking an angel to find you a parking spot close to a store, as this kind of thing will help you build up your confidence. If you are new to spell casting, get into the habit of working with spells, as this will increase your proficiency at them in addition to building up your energy.

Make sure you are in the right frame of mind for the spell. For example, if you are trying to do a positive spell when you are drained of energy, angry, upset, or stressed out, it will probably fail. Wait until your mood improves. Similarly, if you are feeling sick or ill, hold off until you are feeling better.

You must be confident that what you are doing will work, because self-doubt will ruin the spell. Keep spelling, because the more you do something, the more confidence you gain. In the meantime, work on your confidence, self-value, and self-love by making time to meditate on these things. Believe in yourself, and your spells will work. You do need a positive mindset.

Your intent should be clearly spoken without any chance of a different interpretation or any ambiguity. Always use your words in a positive way and not a negative one, so you should say, "I will. This will," and avoid all "No" words or variations. For instance say, "I will get employment. I will be safe in my car when I travel. My relationship will work. This, that or the other thing *will* happen."

Don't do two spells one after another that are asking for opposite or different outcomes, as one or both will end up being cancelled out.

If your spell doesn't work, do not be disheartened about it; just take it as a part of the learning curve. Go back to your spell and re-examine it. Think about why it may not have worked, make the corrections that you feel hindered the spell, pick yourself up, and try again.

Give your spell time to work. I normally give a spell at least three months (unless my spell was based on urgency) before I evaluate whether or not it worked. That tends to be a practical time frame, as indeed spells do tend to manifest more slowly than you would like them to. Another thing is that a spell could manifest in a way that you didn't intend, in which case you will have to do it again in a different way.

designed to fulfill a purpose. Some sigils are personal, and they are charged with personal energy, so they are meant to fulfill our personal desires. Some sigils are charged with energy and used to call on guides or higher beings such as angels, to aid you in some endeavor. In evocation, we use sigils to call forth the entity that we wish to communicate with.

Sigil magic is a very powerful form of enchantment, and yet it is so simple to use that most people have trouble with its simplicity. You would be surprised to know that most people who are successful in their life use this kind of magic in some form or another, although most of them have no idea that they are using sigil magic when they do it. Logos or brand names are typical examples of such sigils.

To perform sigil magic, the first thing you should to do is work out what it is that you want to achieve and write it down. Once it is written down, meditate, and have a clear image in your mind of what you want. Once you have a clear image, take some time to focus on it and see it manifesting itself into reality.

The next step is to create a sigil, and the easiest way to do that is to take a word that represents what you want. Let's say that you want to be happy: write out the word "happiness" on a piece of paper. Take out the vowels, and you will then be left with the letters H,P,P,N,S,S. Play around with these letters until you find that you have drawn an image that resonates with you. This whole creation process of the sigil helps make it stronger because it is your personal sigil, and you are putting your time and energy into it.

Once you have put the letters into an image that resonates with you, focus on it. Be passionate about it, because the more passionate you are, the more energy you'll direct into it, and the faster it will manifest. You can keep the sigil in a pocket or just put it in your wallet or some other place that is personal to you.

The only limitation to sigil magic is your imagination. You can paint images of what you need and surround them as though making a vision board, because anything you put energy into will help bring it into your life. Surround yourself with the energies that you want. You can manifest anything you desire; just remember to be specific and make sure you have a clear image of what you want, and above all—do no harm to anyone or anything.

Nature and Forest Bathing

It is amazing how certain terms suddenly become trendy, and "forest bathing" is one of them. It means being out in nature, and walking or sitting about among

trees and plants. Many witches love connecting to nature, and it's a great way to unwind and meditate. If you haven't tried forest bathing yet, then I suggest you add it to your self-care routine. The trend originated in Japan in the 1980s where it is called *Shinrin Yoku*. It has many health benefits—mental, physical, and spiritual. Forest bathing can reduce stress, improve immunity, lower blood pressure, and aid recovery from illness or trauma. If you have a hard time settling an overactive mind, then sitting or walking in nature can really help clear your mind and energy field. Just thirty minutes a day can really lift your mood.

Time in nature is also good for meditation and visualization, and walking takes your mind off your worries and problems, allowing positive thoughts to surface. It is often a great way to come up with answers to your questions or concerns. You need a clear head and good energy for your spells and rituals to reach their full potential and to achieve the desired outcome.

You could take a journal and write down any thoughts or ideas that come to mind after your outing, and you might even come up with a spell or two.

If you suffer badly from hay fever, you will have to find some other environment to bathe in. Some people go to their local swimming pool and do some leisurely laps, literally bathing in water and forgetting their troubles for a while.

❋ ❋ ❋

DIVINATION

12

Here are some ways to use divination in your spells and rituals. They can connect you with your higher self and open you up to using your intuition, which can often help you gain more insight on situations. You will be able to see yourself and your outer world from a different viewpoint.

Wax Candlemancy

Candlemancy is an ancient form of divination using candlewax. It involves focusing on your question and dripping melted wax into a dish or pan of cold water, then interpreting the symbols and shapes the wax makes as it hardens. This works best with dark-colored candles, or you can use the color candle that represents the spell you are doing at the time. If your question is not related to any of these colors, use a white candle. If you have no question but simply desire a glimpse into your future, you can use white or yellow.

You will need a number of long tapers, eight inches or longer. You will also need a large vessel filled with cold water. This can be made of anything, but glass is best, because it can withstand heat, which plastic can't. You will also need a lighter or a box of long matches.

Put the candles, lighter, or matches, and the bowl of water on a flat surface, such as a table out of doors or an old tray on a kitchen counter.

Sit quietly and calm your mind, think about your question, light the candle, and hold it upright over the water for a moment. When the candle is fully flaming and has begun melting, tilt it and hold it steadily about an inch over the water's surface. The wax will start to drip into the water. As the wax drops, it will form a pattern on the surface of the water. If you are having trouble achieving this, move the candle slowly, allowing the drops to touch one another and so to form a line on the water.

After a few minutes, a definite shape will appear on the water, and you can look at the shape see what it looks like. Pick up the wax shape carefully so as not to break it and turn it over. Does it look the same on the other side or does it look different? Study it to see if it says anything to you symbolically.

What follows are some shapes and patterns that you will often find with this method, along with their traditional meanings. Remember, though, interpretation is a personal thing, so nobody else can tell you exactly how these symbols relate to you, and it is usually the first meaning that comes into your mind that is the correct one.

SPIRALS

This is the most common shape owing to the way the wax rotates on the surface of the water. Spirals represent reincarnation, the universe, the world, or perhaps a previous life.

CIRCLES

Circles represent eternity and fertility, and they can be interpreted according to the question that has been asked. Fertility might represent a new activity, financial security, or even a new baby on the way. It may also signify the successful completion of a project. Eternity may indicate that it will be a long time before something comes to pass.

BROKEN LINES

If the wax drops form into lines but the lines are not connected, it can represent a lack of focus in your life, or muddles in business, or that you are not in control in your life. It can signify forces working against you, but don't take this too literally, because this is often just a warning that you need to make changes to bring order into your life.

DOTS

Unconnected wax drops are sometimes the only thing that lands in your bowl, and this can mean that the problem is too complex for an answer at this time. If you try several times with only dots coming up each time, you're either asking the wrong questions, or you shouldn't be seeking a glimpse into your future at this time. It's probably best to leave the candles and water alone for a while and try a different method.

Here are some symbols you might come across. It will take some practice before you become good at recognizing these.

Image	Interpretation
Airplane	A disappointing trip
Anchor	Your loved one is honest and true
Baby	Problems are coming
Ball or Balloon	Your problem will not last very long
Beans	Money problems
Bed	Rest or a vacation would be good for you
Bells	A wedding
Bird	News will reach you soon
Bridge	Take a chance
Broom	Make a change
Candle	Spiritual growth
Cat	A friend will show their true colors
Chain	Go ahead with your plans
Circle	Reconciliation
Cloud	Something threatens you
Cross	Do not worry, for you are protected
Crown	Sickness

Image	Interpretation
Cup	Quarrels
Dog	Your self-esteem is too low
Ear	New opportunity in your work
Egg	New developments soon
Fan	A surprise is coming
Feather	A problem will be solved
Fish	Betrayal
Ghost	Someone from the past is looking for you
Grass	Good fortune is approaching
Hat	A move
Heart	You will find love
House	Better times are coming
Key	A delay in plans should be expected
Kite	The answer is no
Ladder	Take steps to change your attitude toward an old friend
Leaf or Leaves	Things will change soon
Lion	An unpleasant situation is developing
Moon	More money is coming

Image	Interpretation
Mountain	You will receive help
Pants or Trousers	You will be tempted
Pen	Expect a letter
Pin	Your lover may disappoint you
Pipe	Peace and comfort
Ring	A celebration in the near future
Scissors	Separation
Shoe	Be suspicious of a new acquaintance
Snake	Be on guard against an enemy
Spider's Web	New beginnings
Star	Happiness
Sun	Good fortune
Table	An abundance of blessings
Tree	A good time for new undertakings
Umbrella	Trouble is coming
Walking Stick	Plan to meet friends
Wheel	Someone who has been away will return soon
Witch	Danger will pass you by
Worm	Take care, there will be business troubles

Tarot Cards

Tarot cards are the most popular form of divination, and many psychics, mystics, seers, and witches use them to find answers. Most tarot decks that are used today follow a similar pattern, so their symbolism is universally understood. The cards carry a series of esoteric symbols to convey images, messages, and intuitive feelings. The most common deck in use is the Rider-Waite Tarot.

There are seventy-eight cards in the deck, which comprises twenty-two Major Arcana cards and fifty-six Minor Arcana cards. The Major Arcana depicts the different stages of our life and the journey of the soul in the current lifetime. The journey starts with the card numbered zero, which is called The Fool, and it ends with number twenty-one, which is the World. The fifty-six Minor Arcana cards are less dramatic, and they portray day-to-day events. The word "arcana" means "mystery."

You can teach yourself the tarot by using your own intuition and with plenty of practice, or you can find a good teacher who will help you to understand the cards. When searching for a teacher, always go by recommendation. There are many books that will give you a basic idea, and *In Focus Tarot* is a particularly good one, but there is also a measure of inner guidance and intuitive feeling that you will pick up while using the cards. I use my cards all the time, and I wouldn't be without them. Indeed, I have been reading them for almost thirty years.

The Zodiac and the Tarot

Each sign of the zodiac is linked to one of the tarot cards in the Major Arcana, so it is interesting to know the card for your sign, as this will help you to understand what your soul needs to learn in this lifetime and what you still have to work on and master.

ARIES
March 21–April 19
Your tarot card is The Emperor, and this man will always be there when you need him. This card represents loyalty and the ability to stand by your friends through thick and thin. Like the card, you use your authority and analytical powers to help others and to achieve your own goals.

TAURUS
April 20–May 20
Your tarot card is The Hierophant, and it represents learning from teachers who can help you search for higher truths. Sifting through superficial matters, these learned souls can lead you to the heart of things where profound insights reveal important life lessons.

GEMINI
May 21–June 20
Your tarot card is The Lovers, and for you this often means making a choice between taking the high or low road. This card encourages you to weigh your options carefully and to follow the path dictated by your personal integrity.

CANCER
June 21–July 22
Your tarot card is The Chariot, which involves steering a steady course and rising above life's conflicts. Even though Cancerians seek security, you also love the freedom of the open road where you can use your highly developed intuition for the benefit of yourself and others.

LEO
July 23–August 22
Your tarot card is Strength, which represents your physical strength as well as your emotional, mental, and spiritual prowess. Like the lion depicted on the card, you are blessed with plenty of courage, which helps you overcome problems and obstacles.

VIRGO
August 23–September 22

Your tarot card is The Hermit, and you need to slow down and go within to focus on your purpose in life. The old man shown on the card represents a person who is weary of the outer world, but when he retreats to explore the mysteries of his inner life, he becomes open and innocent like a child.

LIBRA
September 23–October 22

Your tarot card is Justice, asking you to weigh your desires against your needs. In order to reach a fair outcome, you must put your feelings and emotions aside. When you find the answer and reach your decision, you will then be able to serve the greater good.

SCORPIO
October 23–November 21

Your tarot card is the Death card. You welcome transformation, seeking to release your spirit in order to be reborn. Because you can detach yourself from the ties that bind others, it's easy for you to change your identity, making you the mysterious person everyone wants to figure out.

SAGITTARIUS
November 22–December 21

Your tarot card is Temperance, so you are a gifted mediator who is able to find common ground by balancing judgments with genuine understanding and awareness. You can work your way through whatever difficulties get in the way.

CAPRICORN
December 22–January 19

Your tarot card is The Devil; it encourages you to face your shadow-self in order to gather the knowledge necessary for spiritual transformation. It advises you to reflect on any negativity that has made you doubt yourself, swap it for confidence, and hold fast to your highest vision of who you are.

AQUARIUS

January 20–February 18

Your tarot card is The Star, which is also known as the wish card, so you really believe you can achieve your heart's desires. Your job in this world is to persuade others that they can also reach their goals by helping to lead them in the right direction in a spiritual sense.

PISCES

February 19–March 20

Your tarot card is The Moon, so you are a creature of ever-changing moods. The Moon rules emotions, which are your strong point, especially when you use your compassionate nature to tune into others and to help them.

The Pendulum

A favorite divination tool of mine is the pendulum. I use a rose quartz crystal on a chain, but I sometimes use a pendant if I don't have my pendulum handy. You can use anything as long as you feel that it works for you. The pendulum is a tool that helps you to access the collective unconscious and your higher self, and you can get answers to almost anything you come up with. Everyone is capable of working with the pendulum, but it does require practice, and the results you get will reflect your level of spiritual development. You should only use it for good purposes, such as your own well-being and that of others.

You must phrase your question in a form that can be answered with either a yes or a no, although you will sometimes get a "don't know" answer. If you don't get a sensible answer, you should leave it for a couple of weeks before you try again, because it could mean that the outcome is undecided at the present time.

The first thing to do is to determine what each pendulum movement means for you. Sit at a table, place your feet flat on the floor, and rest your elbow on the table. Take hold of the end of the chain between your thumb and index finger, making sure that your upper body and back are straight so the energy can flow freely. Put your other hand flat on the table. Let your breath flow calmly.

Timing the Use

There are two points to take into consideration: the first is to ensure that you won't be interrupted or distracted, and second is not to try this if you are tired or upset.

I tend to hold my pendulum over the center of my other hand, but you must do whatever feels best for you. Now—either speaking out loud or speaking telepathically—ask what your YES will look like. The pendulum may swing from side to side or front to back, or it will go in a clockwise circle or a counterclockwise circle. Whatever it does, this will be your YES.

Now try again, mentally or verbally asking what your NO will look like, and see what the pendulum does.

You can do this a third time and discover what your DON'T KNOW will look like. Now you will be able to find answers to questions.

Don't ask the same question over and over again; just go with the first answer you were given. If you feel that you need to check the answer for reassurance or if you didn't get the answer you hoped for, try again a few days later.

Other Ways of Using a Pendulum

• You can place your pendulum directly over an object, such as water or crystals, and test it for energy.
• You can test the energy of your house and of the place where you sleep.
• You can use a pendulum alongside healing techniques.
• You can use a pendulum for clearing energies and for work with chakras.

• You can use a pendulum with meditation techniques.
• You can buy or make special charts that map out areas for topics like past and future lives, health issues, and more, and use a pendulum to give you guidance on those areas.

Reading Tea Leaves

There is an interesting old tradition called *tasseography*, which is a form of divination that interprets the patterns in tea leaves or coffee grounds—and some modern readers use wine sediment. If you are new to this idea, you may find it useful to try the Nelros Cup, which is a special cup made for divination and marked with the planetary symbols. There are many specialized cups for divination on the market—I have a friend who uses the Taltos Fortune Telling Teacup—and while the designs are usually similar to the Nelros Cup, the symbols are not the same and neither are they in the same positions. I have used the Nelros Cup, so that is what I'll talk about here, but you can likely adapt this information to whatever teacup you buy for yourself.

Preparation

Buy some loose-leaf tea, preferably something like Darjeeling or China tea, which has large leaves. While you can cut open a tea bag and use that, it doesn't work very well because you will be trying to make sense out of tea dust. You can use herbal tea, but make sure there is something to read and not just dusty stuff.

Needless to say, you will need a teapot, but don't use one with a built-in tea strainer, because the whole point of making the tea is to end up with tea leaves in the cup. You will have to drink the tea; you can use milk and sugar or sweetener if you like.

Make your tea and pour it into the cup. Drink the tea slowly while thinking of the things that are on your mind. When you have finished the tea, turn the cup upside down on the saucer, then turn it three times in a clockwise direction and drain away any remaining liquid. Now pick up the cup and turn the handle toward you. The handle represents the person for whom you are doing the reading—maybe yourself or a friend.

The Symbols in the Cup

A Nelros Cup or similar has symbols around it, along with the symbols for the planets, and the saucer has the symbols for the signs of the zodiac. You can use the booklet that comes with your cup and saucer to decipher the meanings of the symbols, or you can work out your own code. They are common symbols that are not hard to understand. For instance, a diamond means good news regarding money, rings suggest marriage, and a snake talks of treachery, and so on. The planets add another dimension to the reading, but you need to know the meanings of the planets in order to make sense of this information.

Start with the symbol under the handle and see if there are tea leaves in it. If so, they are telling you something in connection with the symbol. Look at the planet that sits below the one the leaf is in and see whether that improves the position or turns a good situation bad. For instance, if a tea leaf lands on a picture of two rings, it means marriage. If the planet below it is a nice one like Venus or Jupiter, it talks of a happy marriage, if the planet is Mars, the marriage will be fiery, both in the sense of hot sex or of heated arguments—or both. If the planet is Saturn, the marriage is probably grinding its way to an end. This all takes some imagination (and patience), but it can be great fun.

The Saucer

In theory, you could put the Nelros Cup down on the saucer and see how the symbol and planet line up with the sign of the zodiac, as that would give another level to the reading. However, it would probably be a step too far, causing confusion rather than clarity. Maybe pour a little tea from the teapot into the saucer and see which signs of the zodiac the leaves land on or are close to, and see what these mean for the questioner.

The Runes

The word "rune" means "secret" or "mystery," and rune reading is linked to the ancient north European and Scandinavian alphabets. It is possible that some of the earliest runic inscriptions were not used as a writing system at all but as magical signs to be used as charms and amulets. There is no evidence that runes were used for divination purposes, though.

The name of the ancient alphabet commonly used for divination today is Futhark, so called after its first six letters. The Elder Futhark has twenty-four runes, including one blank tile, which is known as the Wyrd rune. There is also a newer system called Younger Futhark, which has been trimmed down to sixteen runes.

Meanings of the Runes

FEHU

New beginnings, property matters, wealth, luck, responsibility, and creative energy. This rune can be used to draw in the energy that is needed for a given magical operation, or as the moving force behind something you want to accomplish.

URUZ

Positive strength, determination, perseverance, courage, physical health, assertiveness. Use this rune for healing work.

THURISAZ

This is the rune of change and protection, combating any action that is being taken against you, and it represents Thor's hammer, Mjöllnir. One of Odin's sons, Thor was the Norse god of thunder and lightning, and he was a giant and also a warrior god. Take time to think things through before getting involved in anything, and ensure you have performed protection spells.

ANSUZ

This is the rune of communication and words, so it is linked with Odin, the Allfather, the god of wisdom and the god of the runes themselves. This rune can be used to gain knowledge of Odin, the gods, our own ancestors, and ancestral heritage. This is a great rune if you want to study or to teach the magical arts.

RAIDO

This rune is related to travel, so if you have to change location or get around to do your magical work, Raido will help. This helps you to control, take initiatives, put things in order, be the boss, move or remove things, and direct magical energies where they are needed.

KENAZ

Kinship, learning, teaching, quest for knowledge, and passing knowledge on. Also obtaining occult knowledge from other planes; use for astral or shamanic travel; exposing what is hidden.

GEBO

Reconciles two opposed or complementary forces. Use Gebo to bind something that might otherwise fall apart or to give blessings.

WUNJO

To realize true will, wishing, and hoping. Combines well with Raido (ability to control).

HAGALAZ

This rune creates confusion and disruption. It can be used as a barrier spell that will prevent someone from harming you or from harming others.

NAUTHIZ
This is excellent for defensive magic, as in restraining or restricting someone else's magickal attack against you. It can be used to stop someone else's bad intentions in any sphere of life.

ISA
Defense by blocking, that is, placing barriers in the path of an opponent or competitor.

JERA
Creates positive, lasting change in a situation. Works well in all matters involving time.

EIHWAZ
Use this rune in situations that demand energy, courage, and get-up-and-go, such as searching for a job or looking for somewhere to live.

PERTHO
Use in regression work. This rune can put you in touch with the Norns, three sisters in Norse mythology who are associated with fate—the past, the present, and the future.

ALGIZ
Use Algiz to invoke divine protection. It acts as a shielding device, especially where backlash is a consideration. It can be applied to the four corners of a space as a protective sigil, much like a pentagram but with a more defensive effect.

SOWELO
Contributes strength to any healing spell. Reinforces other runes with solar energy, and it centers and directs any efforts you make or any magic rituals that you perform.

Bind-Runes

·······•••◆◆◆•••·······

Bind-runes are two or more runes put together, which can create a third outcome. Bind-runes are stronger together than the runes would be individually.

TIWAZ

This is a warrior rune, as it is associated with Tyr, the Norse god of war and battle. Tempered with a sense of justice, Tyr also represented law and order, and this rune helps you obtain justice, but only if you have right on your side. It won't work if you are guilty or if you try to pervert the course of justice. A combination of Tiwaz and Raido in a bind-rune can help you win a court case.

BERKANA

Important in feminine mysteries. Regenerates the forces of nature, growth of vegetation, strong shamanic connections. Use Berkana to alleviate problems with menstrual periods, pregnancy, and childbirth.

EHWAZ

This helps you move on, change address, face up to change, have courage to make a change. It can help to create links between people or split them apart.

MANNAZ

Useful when communication is needed. It helps someone pass exams or win legal disputes. It can be used to arbitrate or mediate in a conflict. If used with Ansuz in a bind-rune, it can help with any form of communication.

LAGUZ

To combat sorcery, but the rune can also be used to attract love. Imagine Laguz on your forehead when asking for something, and as long as what you are asking for is reasonable, you should get a positive response.

INGUZ

This is the rune of conception and fertility. It is named for the god Ing, who is the Danish/Anglo-Saxon god of agriculture and fertility. Use this when you need to bind someone or something and stop them from wandering off. It also makes a great doorway to the astral realm, so project this onto an imaginary door or curtain if you want to travel in this way.

OTHILA

For establishing, centering, and grounding. It can be used to invoke Odin. It creates a sense of belonging and togetherness in groups that work together, and binds people together when working for a common goal.

DAGAZ

This can exclude something or render it invisible. Use this rune when you want to put something "outside" or out of the way. You could also use this rune as a kind of cloak of invisibility; for example, you can envelop yourself in the rune if you want to go somewhere unnoticed. This is a lucky rune, so it is useful when you need a change of luck.

How to Read the Runes

There are many different ways of casting and reading the runes, and there are plenty of books available that will show you everything in detail. You can start, though, with three easy castings that will allow you to begin working with them right away, which will encourage you to get used to their energies and how they operate.

When I am going to read the runes, I spread out my rune cloth, then I pour the rune stones onto the cloth, and stir them around clockwise, using my right hand. I concentrate on the question I want to ask, and, with my eyes closed, I pick up a few runes at random and prepare to read them. It is important to have a specific question in mind when reading the runes. A *yes* or *no* reading is the easiest for a beginner to use until you get the hang of it.

CAST ONE RUNE

This is great for a daily casting, and it is an easy one to use as a guide for your day. Think of your question and draw one rune. Say you draw Ansuz and it is upright rather than reversed or facedown. I see this as saying that communication is very important for you on this day, so be sure to explain yourself clearly, speak up when necessary, and listen to what others have to say.

CAST THREE RUNES

Think of your question and draw three runes. The first rune will be the *overview*, giving a general background to your question. The second rune is the *course of action*, which tells you what your options are and what you might want to do. The third rune is the *outcome*.

DRAWING THREE RUNES FOR YES OR NO

This cast allows you to ask questions that can be answered with a yes or no. Ask your question and draw three runes. Take note of how many runes are upright or reversed. Upright runes are positive, while those that are reversed or facedown are negative.

When all three runes are positive, the answer is definitely *yes*. When all three runes are negative, the answer is definitely *no*, but the meanings of the runes will usually tell you why the reading is positive or negative, and what you could do to increase your chances of success.

When two runes are positive and one is negative, the answer will still be *yes*, but the situation may not meet your expectations.

When two runes are negative and one is positive, the answer is *no*, but it may turn out not to be too bad in the end.

Not all the runes can be reversed, as some look the same either way up, and any of these can be treated as negative runes.

For those who use the blank rune, this next part is important. If the blank rune appears in your yes or no draw, it means you are probably better off not knowing the answer at that point in time. Wait a day and ask the question again. If the blank rune appears again, then you really should give up asking the question, because you are simply not meant to know the answer.

CONCLUSION

I hope as you have reached the end of this book that it has inspired you to carry on along the Wiccan path and to enjoy learning more about yourself while expanding your knowledge. Now that you understand the principles and practices of Wicca, you can create a more magical and powerful way of living. By integrating some of the rituals into your life, you can do things like increasing your chances of finding a loving relationship, making good friends, having a peaceful and pleasant place to live, creating abundance, spending more time in nature, working with the elements, and focusing inward.

When you are ready to learn, the teacher often appears either in physical or spiritual form to help you on your life journey. Take time to connect to your ancestors and spirit guides and to create and manifest new opportunities and events. Just spend a little quiet time alone to focus inward to understand what is right for you and what resonates with you.

I wish you all the luck on your path—may it bring peace and enrich your life.

ABOUT THE AUTHOR

Tracie Long began to see and hear spirits when she was about six years old, and she went through her teens and twenties feeling very different from most people. It wasn't until she was in her early thirties that she finally embraced her gift. Like many psychics and mediums, she has spent a long time practicing and studying, and she has now been working in the mind, body, spirit industry for almost thirty years.

Tracie specializes in tarot, angels, spiritual development, meditation, shamanic healing and coaching, and moon cycles. She has worked with sensitive children, and run a few paranormal investigations, but today she is most often called upon to help spirits who are stuck or causing problems for families to pass over. She also tutors alongside the Spiritual Workers Association, was a chairwoman of the British Astrological and Psychic Society from 2017 to 2018, has a BTEC in business management, and, in 2011, completed a teaching degree.

Index

IMAGE CREDITS

Cover: sun © Anastasia Mazeina/Shutterstock; moon © Andreea Eremia/Shutterstock; stars © LeKodesign/Shutterstock; frame © painterr/Shutterstock; texture © Andrius_Saz/Shutterstock

Poster: frame © painterr/Shutterstock; texture © Andrius_Saz; book, wand, broom © Artur Balytskyi/Shutterstock; athame © Artinblackink/Shutterstock; pentacle © Vlada Young/Shutterstock; censer, candle © zhekakopylov/Shutterstock; chalice © 2 Rivers/Shutterstock; bolline © Morphart Creation/Shutterstock; cauldron © Alexander_P/Shutterstock; bell © Santi0103/Shutterstock

Interior:
Glyphs on 128 and 129 by Terry Marks

Runes on 133, 134, 135, 136, 137 by Tandem Books

Shutterstock: 7, 10, 25, 37 (center) © Morphart Creation; geometric shape on 8, 20, 28, 32, 44, 50, 68, 82, 88, 94, 104, 120 © acid2728k; stars on 8, 20, 28, 32, 44, 50, 68, 76, 82, 88, 94, 104, 120 © EssentiallyNomadic; 9, 13 © Gorbash Varvara; 11 © Everett Collection; 14, 15 © Nadin Koryukova; 16 (bottom) © Hoika Mikhail; 16 (top) © Eroshka; 17 © P.S.Art-Design-Studio; 18 (bottom), 41 © Kseniakrop; 18 (top) © Epine; 19 (bottom), 46 © bogadeva1983; 19 (top) © Marzufello; 21, 26 © Zvereva Yana; 22 © Marketa Kuchynkova; 23 © robin.ph; 24, 38 (bottom), 110 © andrey oleynik; 27 © juliawhite; 29 (bottom) © Tata Donets; 29 (center) © CoolVectorStock; 29 (top) © konstantinks; 30 (cornucopia) © S_O_Va; 30 (Green Man) © patrimonio designs ltd; 30 (hexagram) © Pyty; 30 (threes) © ASAG Studio; 30 (wheel) © jisoo_88; 31 (maze) © Vladvm; 31 (triple moon) © 4LUCK; 31 (triquetra) © Tasha Vector; 31 (web) © Arcady; 33, 36 (top), 37 (top), 132 (bottom) © Artur Balytskyi; 34 (book) © LAATA9; 34 (athame) © Artinblackink; 35 © Vlada Young; 36 (bottom) © 2 Rivers; 36 (center) © zhekakopylov; 37 (bottom), 43 © Alexander_P; 38 (top) © Santi0103; 39 © AlexHliv; 42 © tsaplia; 45 © dariautumn; 47, 131 © mart; 48 © Drekhann; 51 © paw; 53 © NataLima; 56 © Lisla; 58, 60 © Olha Saiuk; 61 © pikepicture; 63 © nfsstudio; 64, 109 © Bodor Tivadar; 65 © makeevadecor; 72 © galacticus; 74, 75 © sini4ka; 76 © ekosuwandono; 80 © Creativika Graphics; 83, 84, 85, 86, 117 © Peratek; 87 © Vasya Kobelev; 89 © Babich Alexander; 92 © Purebo; 98 © Dariia Baranova; 99, 132 (top) © MoreVector; 126 © Wonder-studio; 139 © Bourbon-88; 103, 114 © N_Melanchenko; 129 (pendulum) © vip2807; 137 (pouch) © Svetlana Filimonova